PROBLEMS AND SOLUTIONS IN FINANCIAL MANAGEMENT- Step By Step Approach

RAJNI KANT RAJHANS

Copyright © 2015 Rajni Kant Rajhans

All rights reserved.

ISBN: 1480048119
ISBN-13: 978-1480048119

ACKNOWLEDGMENTS & DEDICATION

First and foremost, I would like to thank my parents and grandparents for allowing me to pursue my ambitions throughout my childhood. I also would like to thank my wife Aditi Rajhans for always motivating and standing beside me throughout my career. She always celebrates my achievements and discusses my current research and future plans. I also thank my doll (daughter) "Reeti Rajhans" for always making me unstressed with her cute smile. She is the best daughter in the world. I can't forget to mention my younger brother Avni Kant Rajhans here. He is my IT hand. His continuous support and motivation helped me a lot in completing this book. I also thank to my in-laws who supported me unconditionally in pursuing my career. I dedicate this book to all of them.

My colleagues, especially Dr. Ashutosh Kumar who help me always with their guidance and all supports. I would like to acknowledge the contribution of my students Suryansh and Supriya in completing this book.

CONTENTS

1 Time Value of Money   Pg 1-30

2 Risk and Return   Pg 31-54

3 Valuation of Equity   Pg 55-76

4 Valuation of Bond   Pg 77-110

5 Cost of Capital   Pg 110-122

6 Capital Budgeting   Pg 123-141

1 TIME VALUE OF MONEY

Learning Objective: To enable reader to understand the practical applications of time value of money and related concepts like: compounding, discounting etc.

- Time Value of Money:- "A dollar (rupee) today worth more than a dollar (rupee) tomorrow". This is because of: risk associated, consumption preference and investment options available on today's money.
- Future Value:- The value of a rupee (dollar) invested today for a time period 't' at a rate of interest of 'r%'.

$$\text{Future Value (FV)} = P(1 + r/100)^t$$

If rate of interest is calculated at a frequency of f then,

$$FV = P[1 + r/(f \times 100)]^{f \times t}$$

- Annuity:- It is inflows (or Outflows) of a particular sum of money at a fixed frequency for a particular time period.

Note: The inflows (Outflows) can be at the beginning of the year or can be at the end of the year.

  o If the inflows (Outflows) are at the beginning of the period, it is known as Annuity Due.
  o If the inflows (Outflows) are at the end of the period, it is known as Deferred annuity.

- Present Value:-It is the amount that should be invested today to have a particular return (future value) after a specified period. Present value of a single cash flow after time 't' is :

✓ If F_t is the amount to be received after time 't' and the expected rate of interest is r% per annum, present value of F_t can be calculated as:

$$P = F_t/(1+r/100)^t$$

- **Present Value of Annuity:**

$$P = A/r\,[1 - 1/(1+r)^t]$$

- Perpetuity:- is an annuity having infinite life. Present value of annuity = A/r
- Annuity Due:- is an annuity having inflows(or outflows) starting at the beginning of the period.

Future Value of Annuity Due = Future Value of Annuity × (1+r) → Interest of 1st period.

*Effective Interest Rate:- If frequency of compounding is more than one in a year, the rate of return is higher than nominal rate of interest, this rate of interest is known as effective rate of interest.

*Continuous Compounding: Frequency of compounding is considered at the smallest fraction of time.

TYPE I: Problems on Time Value of Money:- Future Value

Step I: Identify the sum that is being invested. (P)

Step II: Identify the rate of interest. (r)

Step III: Identify the time period of investment. (t)

Step IV: Apply the formula:

FV = P[1+ r/100]^t

Ex:- Ram wants to invest $ 5000 for a period of 5 Years The rate of interest is 10% per annum (p.a.). Find the sum of money Ram will get after 5 Years

Solution:

Step I: Identify the sum that is being invested. P = $ 5000

Step II: Identify the rate of interest. r = 10% p.a.

Step III: Identify the time period of investment. t= 5 Years

Step IV: Apply the formula:

FV = P[1+ r/100]^t = 5000 [1+ 10/100]^5= $ 8052.55

PRACTICE PROBLEMS:

Q1. Mr. A invested $ 10,000 in a fixed deposit having rate of interest of 5% per annum for 10 Years How much amount will he get after 10 Years?

Q2. Mr. B wants to have a sum of $ 5800 after 2 Years He has two investment options to select one for his investment objective:

Investment Option 1: Rate of interest of 8% p.a.

Investment Option 2: Rate of interest of 6% p.a.

If Mr. B has $ 5000 to invest for 2 Years, which investment option will meet his objective?

TYPE II: Problems on Future Value for different frequency of

compounding

Step I: Identify the frequency of compounding i.e. f.

Step II: Multiply the time given with frequency. (t×f).

Step III: Divide the rate of interest given with frequency. (r/f)

Step IV: Apply the formula:

$FV = P[1+r/(100 \times f)]^{(t \times f)}$

Q1. Shyam wants to calculate how much money he will get after 2 Years at a rate of interest of 10% p.a. compounded half-yearly on a sum of money of $ 5000?

Solution: Step I: Identify the frequency of compounding i.e. f = half-yearly = 2 times in a year= 2.

Step II: Multiply the time given with frequency. t×f = 2 Years× 2 = 4 periods

Step III: Divide the rate of interest given with frequency. r/f = 10% / 2 = 5 % per period.

Step IV: Apply the formula:

$FV = P[1+r/(100 \times f)]^{(t \times f)} = 5000[1+ 10/(100 \times 2)]^4 = 5000[1.05]^4 = $ $ 6077.53$

PRACTICE PROBLEMS:

Q1. Branch Manager of S.B.I. has to answer question of his client "how much will I get after 2 Years by investing $ 10,000 in your bank?" The rate of interest S.B.I. offers is 5% p.a. compounded quarterly.

Q2. Which of the two investments is better?

Option I: Investment of $ 1000 for 2 Years at 10 % p.a. compounded annually.

Option II: Investment of $ 900 for 2 Years at 15.36% p.a. compounded semi-annually.

Q3. How much money you will get if invested at 8% p.a. compounded monthly? The investment amount is $ 1000 for 10 Years

Q4. How much money will you get after 3 Years if invested $ 2000 today at 4 % p.a. compounded weekly?

TYPE III: Problems on Present Value

Step I: Identify the amount needed/ generated after given time. (FV)

Step II: Identify the rate of interest given. (r)

Step III: Identify the period after which the demand/ need of sum (money) is. (t)

Step IV: Apply the formula:

$P = F_t / (1+ r)^t$

Example:- How much money should you invest today to have a sum of $ 1 million after 5 Years for your marriage purpose if rate of interest is 5% p.a. compounded annually?

Solution:

Step I: Identify the amount needed/ generated after given time. FV = $ 1 million

Step II: Identify the rate of interest given. r = 5 % p.a.

Step III: Identify the period after which the demand/ need of sum (money) is. t =5 Years

Step IV: Apply the formula:

$P = F_t / (1+ r)^t = 1$ million$/ (1.05)^5 = \$ 783526.17$

PRACTICE PROBLEMS:

Q1. Mr. Raghu will be retiring after 30 Years He wants to invest an amount which can generate a sum of $ 10 million. The rate of interest is 10 % p.a. compounded annually. Find the amount of investment required?

Q2. Ms. Rachna wants to buy a car of $ 500000 after 5 Years How much should she invest today to fulfill the requirement if rate of interest is 20% p.a.?

Q3. Find present value of following cash flow:

Year	0	1	2	3
Cash flow ($)	7000	2000	8000	9000

[Hint: Take different period as a single time horizon]

TYPE IV: Problems on effective rate of interest

Step I: Identify the given rate of interest. (r)

Step II: Identify the frequency at which interest is calculated. (f)

Step III: Divide the rate of interest by frequency and multiply with the time period of investment. (r/ f   &   t× f)

Step IV: Apply the formula:

$r_{effective} = [1+r/f]^{(t \times f)} - 1$

Example: Find the effective rate of interest if interest is calculated at 9% p.a. compounded quarterly for 1 year?

Step I: Identify the given rate of interest. r = 9%

Step II: Identify the frequency at which interest is calculated. f = quarterly = 4 times in a year= 4

Step III: Divide the rate of interest by frequency and multiply with the time period of investment. r/ f = 9%/ 4 = 2.25%   &   t× f = 1 Years× 4 = 4 period.

Step IV: Apply the formula:

$r_{effective} = [1+r/f]^{(t \times f)} - 1 = [1+2.25\%]^4 - 1 = [1.0225]^4 - 1 = 9.03\%$.

PRACTICE PROBLEMS:

Q1. Find the effective rate of interest, if rate of interest is 8% p.a. compounded monthly?

Q2. Find the effective rate of interest in the following given conditions:

a). r = 5% p.a. compounded half-yearly.

b). r= 10% p.a. compounded weekly.

c). r= 1% p.a. compounded daily.

TYPE V: Problems on Future value of annuity

Step I: Identify the amount of inflow/outflow. (A)

Step II: Identify the rate of interest. (r)

Step III: Identify the frequency of compounding. (f).

Step IV: If frequency of compounding is not annual, find the effective rate of interest.

Step V: Identify the total number of inflows/ outflows. (t)

Step VI: Apply the formula:

$FV = A/r [(1+r)^t - 1]$

Example 1: Find the maturity value of a yearly installment of $ 100 for 24 Years if rate of interest is 5% p.a.

Step I: Identify the amount of inflow/outflow. A = $ 100.

Step II: Identify the rate of interest. r = 5% p.a.

Step III: Identify the frequency of compounding. f = annual

Step IV: If frequency of compounding is not annual, find the effective rate of interest. **(Not applicable in this case)**

Step V: Identify the total number of inflows/ outflows. t=24

Step VI: Apply the formula:

$FV = A [(1+r)^t - 1] / r = 100 \times [1.05^{24} - 1] / 0.05 = \$ 4450.2$

Example 2: Find the maturity value of a monthly installment of $ 100 for 12 months if rate of interest is 5% p.a. compounded annually.

Step I: Identify the amount of inflow/outflow. A = $ 100.

Step II: Identify the rate of interest. r = 5% p.a.

Step III: Identify the frequency of compounding. f = annual

Step IV: If frequency of compounding is not annual, find the effective rate of interest.

As installment payment is in monthly frequency, hence, we need to find effective rate of interest as

$r_{effective} = [1+r]^{1/12} - 1 = [1+5\%]^{1/12} - 1 = [1.05]^{1/12} - 1 = 0.407\%$.

Step V: Identify the total number of inflows/ outflows. t=12

Step VI: Apply the formula:

FV = A [$(1+r/f)^{t \times f} - 1$] /(r/f) = $100 \times [1.00407^{12} - 1]/ 0.00407$ = $ 1227.23

PRACTICE PROBLEMS:

Q1. Find the future value of an annuity paying $ 1000 every year for 10 Years. The rate of interest is 6% p.a. compounded annually. Cash outflows occur at the end of each period.

Q2. Find the future value of an annuity paying $ 1000 every year for 10 Years. The rate of interest is 6% p.a. compounded annually. Cash outflows occur at the beginning of each period.

TYPE VI: Problems on Present value of annuity

Step I: Identify the amount of inflows /outflows.

Step II: Identify the discounting rate i.e. rate of interest.

Step III: Identify time (t) for which cash flows will be generated.

Step IV: Apply the formula:

$PV = A[(1+r)^t - 1]/(r \times (1+r)^t)$

Q1. How much you should invest today in lump–sum so that you can get a monthly income of $1000 for next 10 years. The rate of interest is 12% p.a.

Solution:

Step I: Inflow amount (A) = $1000 monthly.

Step II: Rate of interest (r) = 12 % p.a. = $(1.12)^{(1/12)}$ = 0.94 % per month

Step III: time period (t) = 10 Years = 120 months.

Step IV: Using formula:

$PV = A[(1+r)^t - 1]/(r \times (1+r)^t) = 1000 [(1.0094)^{120} - 1]/(0.0094 \times (1.0094)^{120}] = \$71767$

Hence, an amount of $71767 will have to be deposited today.

Q2. How much should you invest today in lump sum to generate a monthly cash inflow of $100 for 2 Years; if rate of interest is 10% p.a. compounded half-yearly?

Solution:

Step I: Cash inflow (A) = $100 per month.

Step II: rate of interest (r) = 10% p.a. compounded half-yearly = $(1+0.1/2)^2 - 1$ = 10.25% p.a.

Step III: Hence, monthly rate of interest = $(1.1025)^{1/12} - 1$ = 0.816% p.m.

Step IV: time (t) = 2 Years = 24 months

Step V: Apply the formula:

P.V = A $[(1+r)^t-1]/(r \times (1+r)^t)$ = $100[1/(0.00816) - 1/(0.00816 \times (1.00816)^{24})]$ = $ 2171.6

Type VII: Problems on Perpetuity

Step I: Identify cash inflow/ outflow installments (A).

Step II: Identify rate of interest (r).

Step III: Apply the formula:

PV of annuity = A/r.

Q1. How much you should invest today to earn an installment of $ 100 for infinite life, if rate of interest is 8% p.a.?

Solution:

Step I: Installment (A) = $ 100.

Step II: rate of interest(r) = 8% p.a.

Step III: Apply the formula:

PV of annuity = A/r = 100/0.08 = $1250.

Q2. How much should you invest today to earn an installment of $100 for infinite period; if rate of interest is 8% p.a. compounded monthly?

Solution:

This is different from Q1 only in terms of compounding. Hence, we will have to find effective rate of interest.

$r_{eff} = (1+0.08/12)^{12}-1 = 8.3$ % p.a.

Hence, using same steps and formula, we have

P.V of annuity = A/r = 100/0.083 = $ 1204.8

Type VIII: Problems on Annuity Due

Note: Follow the same steps as of annuity. Just change the formula as:

F.V. of annuity due = A/r $[(1+r)^t-1]$ $(1+r)$

Ex.1: Find the maturity value of a yearly installment of $ 100 paid at the beginning of the period for 24 Years; if rate of interest is 5% p.a.

Solution:

F.V. of annuity Due = A/r $[(1+r)^t-1]$ $(1+r)$

Given A= $ 100, t=24 Years, r= 5% p.a.

F.V = $100[(1.05)^{24} -1] (1.05)/0.05 = \$ 4672.71$

Concept: We are multiplying by (1+r) to the formula of future value of annuity because payment is being done at the beginning of the period and hence, interest will be calculated on this amount as well.

Type IX: Problems on continuous compounding

Step I: Identify the amount of investment (A).

Step II: Identify rate of interest (r).

Step III: Identify time (t).

Step IV: Use the formula:

Future Value $(F_t) = A \times e^{rt}$

Ex1: You deposited $100 in a scheme of S.B.I for 20 Years which offer continuous compounding at a rate of 5% p.a. How much amount will you get on maturity?

Solution:

Step I: Amount (A) = $100.

Step II: rate of interest (r) = 5% p.a.

Step III: time (t) = 20 Years

Step IV: Future Value $(F_t) = A \times e^{rt} = 100 \, (2.71)^{(0.05 \times 20)} = \$ \, 271$

More Problems for Practice

Q1. You have taken an education loan of $ 500000 to be repaid in 10 equal installments (principal + interest). The rate of interest is 10% p.a. Find the amount of installment.

Q2. Find the present value of $ 100000 receivable after 20 Years if rate of interest is 5% p.a.

Q3. Find rate of interest at which invested amount will become double in 10 Years

Q4. Find rate of interest at which invested amount will become triple in 8 Years

Q5. Find rate of interest you should earn to double your money in 9 Years

Q6. You invest $ 1000 every month in a retirement fund for 30 Years. If rate of interest offered is 7 % per annum, what amount will you receive after 30 Years?

Q7. You have invested a lump sum of $1000000 in a fund that offers a rate of interest of 8 % p.a. compounded half-yearly. If you want to withdraw this amount in 10 Years, what monthly installment will you receive?

Q8. If Harish wants to accumulate $ 100,000 in 10 Years, how much must he deposit today in an account that pays an annual interest rate of 10%?

Q9. How many Years will it take for $ 100,000 to become $ 400,000 if it is invested in an account with an annual interest rate of 10%?

Q10. How many Years will it take for $ 16,000 to grow to be $ 60,000 if it is invested in an account with an annual interest rate of

8%?

Q11. How many Years will it take for $ 36,000 to become $ 400,000 if it is invested in an account with an annual interest rate of 15%?

Q12. If interest rate is paid at 5 % per annum compounded monthly, compute the effective rate of interest.

Q13. If interest rate is paid at 5 % per annum compounded quarterly, compute the effective rate of interest.

Q14. If interest rate is paid at 10 % per annum compounded half-yearly, compute the effective rate of interest.

Q15. Compute present value of a series of three cash-outflows of $ 1000 each. Each cash-flow is at an interval of 1 year (at the beginning), discount rate is 10%. Compute present value under following conditions:

a). First cash-flow occurs today.

b). First cash flow occurs after 1 year

[Hint: Draw time-time for this question]

Q16. You are told that if you invest $ 10,000 per year for 10 Years (all payments made at the beginning of each year) you will get a sum assured of $ 400,000 at the end of the period. What annual rate of return is the investment offering?

Q17. SBI bank offers 9.75% nominal interest for a five year fixed deposit to senior citizens. If the compounding is done quarterly, then calculate effective annual rate of interest.

Q18. Mr. A deposits $500 at the end of every month in a bank for 10 year If the interest rate offered by bank is 9.25% p.a.

compounded monthly, calculate the accumulated sum A will get after 10 Years

[Hint: First calculate effective rate of interest i.e. 9.65%, then apply the formula of annuity.]

Q19. Mr. B takes a loan of $ 1,00,000 today and return $ 1,18,800 after 5 years to clear off the loan, what effective annual interest rate is paid by Mr. B?.

Q20. In how much time $ 1 becomes $ 2 at 9% rate of interest compounded annually?

Q21. In how much period $ 1 becomes $ 3 at 9% rate of interest compounded annually?

Q22. In how much period $ 1 becomes $ 3 at 9% rate of interest compounded half-yearly?

Q23. In how much period $ 1 becomes $ 2 at 9% rate of interest compounded half-yearly?

Q24. In how much period $ 1 becomes $ 2 at 9% rate of interest compounded quarterly?

Q25. In how much period $ 1 becomes $ 3 at 9% rate of interest compounded quarterly?

Q26. Mr. A deposits $ 1000 at the end of every month in a bank for 5 years If the interest rate offered by bank is 9 % p.a. compounded yearly, calculate the accumulated sum A will get after 5 years.

Q27. Mr. A deposits $ 500 at the end of every month in a bank for 10 Years If the interest rate offered by bank is 9.25% p.a. compounded quarterly, calculate the accumulated sum A will get after 10 Years

Q28. Mr. A deposits $ 500 at the beginning of every month in a bank for 10 Years If the interest rate offered by bank is 9.25% p.a. compounded monthly, calculate the accumulated sum A will get after 10 Years.

SOLUTIONS OF PRACTICE PROBLEMS

TYPE I:

Q1. **Step I:** Sum being invested (P) = Rs. 10,000

Step II: Rate of Interest (r) = 5%

Step III: Time of investment (t) = 10 years

Step IV: Apply the formula:-

$$FV = P\left[1 + \frac{r}{100}\right]^t$$

$$= 10,000\left[1 + \frac{5}{100}\right]^{10}$$

= Rs. 16288.95

Hence, Mr. A will get Rs. 16,288.95 after 10 years.

Q2. Calculation for option 1:

Step I: Sum being invested (P) = Rs. 5000

Step II: Rate of Interest (r) = 8%

Step III: Time of investment (t) = 2 years

Step IV: Apply the formula:-

$$FV = P\left[1 + \frac{r}{100}\right]^t$$

$$= 5000\left[1 + \frac{8}{100}\right]^2$$

=> FV = Rs. 5832.

Calculation for option 2:

Step I: Sum being invested (P) = Rs. 5000

Step II: Rate of Interest (r) = 6%

Step III: Time of investment (t) = 2 years

Step IV: Apply the formula:-

$$FV = P\left[1 + \frac{r}{100}\right]^t$$

$$= 5000\left[1 + \frac{6}{100}\right]^2$$

= Rs. 5618

Since, Mr. B needs Rs. 5800 and hence option 1 will meet his objective.

TYPE II:

Q1. **Step I:** Frequency (f) = 4

Step II: Period of Investment = 2 years

= 2 x 4 quarters

= 8 quarters

Step III: $\dfrac{\text{Rate}}{f} = \dfrac{5\%}{4} = 1.25\%$ quarterly

Step IV: Apply the formula:

$$FV = P\left[1 + \dfrac{r}{f \times 100}\right]^{t \times f}$$

$$= 10{,}000\left[1 + \dfrac{5}{4 \times 100}\right]^{2 \times 4}$$

$\Rightarrow FV = $ Rs. 11,044.86

Hence, client will get Rs. 11,044.86 after 2 years.

Q2. Calculation for option 1:-

Step I: Frequency (f) = 1

Step II: Period of Investment = 2 years

Step III: $\dfrac{\text{Rate}}{f} = \dfrac{10\%}{1} = 10\%$

Step IV: Apply the formula:

$$FV = P\left[1 + \dfrac{r}{f \times 100}\right]^{t \times f}$$

$$= 1000\left[1 + \dfrac{10}{1 \times 100}\right]^{2 \times 1}$$

$\Rightarrow FV = $ Rs. 1210.

Calculation for option 2:-

Step I: Frequency (f) = 2

Step II: Period of Investment = 2 years

= 2 x 2 semi annual

= 4 semi-annual

Step III: $\dfrac{\text{Rate}}{f} = \dfrac{15.36\%}{2} = 7.68\%$ semi - annual

Step IV: Apply the formula:

$$FV = P\left[1 + \dfrac{r}{f \times 100}\right]^{t \times f}$$

$$= 900\left[1 + \dfrac{15.36}{2 \times 100}\right]^{2 \times 2}$$

FV = Rs. 1209.99 ≈ Rs. 1210.

Hence, FV = Rs. 1210.

Since, in both the options; FV is coming equal and hence both the options are equal in terms of return.

Q3. **Step I:** Frequency (f) = 2

Step II: Time of Investment = 10 years

= 10 x 12 months

= 120 months

Step III: $\dfrac{\text{Rate}}{f} = \dfrac{8\%}{12} = 0.67\%$ per month

Step IV: Apply the formula:

$$FV = P\left[1 + \dfrac{r}{f \times 100}\right]^{t \times f}$$

$$= 1000\left[1 + \dfrac{8}{12 \times 100}\right]^{10 \times 12}$$

FV = Rs. 2219.64.

Therefore, value of investment after 2 years will be Rs. 2219.64

Q4. **Step I:** Frequency (f) = 52 (since there are 52 weeks in a year)

Step II: Period of Investment = 3 years

= 3 x 52 weeks

Step III: $\dfrac{\text{Rate}}{f} = \dfrac{4\%}{52}$ per week

Step IV: Apply the formula:

$$FV = P\left[1 + \dfrac{r}{f \times 100}\right]^{t \times f}$$

$$= 2000\left[1 + \dfrac{4}{52 \times 100}\right]^{3 \times 52}$$

FV = Rs. 2254.89

Hence, value of investment after 3 years = Rs. 2254.89

TYPE III:

Q1. Step I: Amount needed (FV) = Rs. 100 lakh.

Step II: Rate of interest (r) = 10% p.a.

Step III: t = 30 years.

Step IV: Apply the formula:-

$$PV = \frac{FV}{\left[1 + \frac{r}{100}\right]^t}$$

$$= \frac{100 \text{ lakh}}{\left[1 + \frac{10}{100}\right]^{30}}$$

= Rs. 5,73,085.53

Hence, amount needed to invest = Rs. 5,73,085.53.

Q2. Step I: Amount needed (FV) = Rs. 5 lakh.

Step II: Rate of interest (r) = 20% p.a.

Step III: t = 5 years.

Step IV: Apply the formula:-

$$PV = \frac{FV}{\left[1 + \frac{r}{100}\right]^t}$$

$$= \frac{5 \, lakh}{\left[1 + \frac{20}{100}\right]^5}$$

$= Rs.\ 2,00,938.79$

Hence, amount needed to invest = Rs. 2,00,938.79.

Q3. STEP I: Amount needed year wise :

Year	0	1	2	3
Amount	7,000	2,000	8,000	9,000

STEP II: Apply formula for each cash flow	$\dfrac{7000}{\left[1+\dfrac{10}{100}\right]^0}$	$\dfrac{2000}{\left[1+\dfrac{10}{100}\right]^1}$	$\dfrac{3000}{\left[1+\dfrac{10}{100}\right]^2}$	$\dfrac{9000}{\left[1+\dfrac{10}{100}\right]^3}$
Hence, present values	7000	1818.18	6611.57	6761.83

TYPE IV:

Q1. **Step I:** Given rate = 8%

Step II: Frequency = Monthly = 12 times in a year

Step III: $\dfrac{Rate}{f} = \dfrac{8\%}{12}$ per month

Step IV: Apply the formula:

$$r_{effective} = \left[1 + \frac{r}{f}\right]^{t \times f} - 1$$

$$= \left[1 + \frac{8}{12 \times 100}\right]^{1 \times 12} - 1$$

$$= 0.083$$

Hence, effective rate of interest = 8.3%. per annum.

Q2. (a) Step I: Given rate = 5%

Step II: Frequency = Half-yearly = 2 times in a year

Step III: $\dfrac{\text{Rate}}{f} = \dfrac{5\%}{2}$ per half - year

Step IV: Apply the formula:

$$r_{effective} = \left[1 + \frac{r}{f}\right]^{t \times f} - 1$$

$$= \left[1 + \frac{5}{2 \times 100}\right]^{1 \times 2} - 1$$

$$= 0.056$$

Hence, effective rate of interest = 5.6%. per annum.

(b) Step I: Given rate = 10%

Step II: Frequency (f) = 52   [as it is weekly]

Step III: $\dfrac{\text{Rate}}{f} = \dfrac{10\%}{52}$

Step IV: Apply the formula:

$$r_{\text{effective}} = \left[1 + \dfrac{r}{f}\right]^{t \times f} - 1$$

$$= \left[1 + \dfrac{10}{52 \times 100}\right]^{1 \times 52} - 1$$

$$= 0.10506$$

$r_{\text{effective}} = 10.506\%$

Hence, effective rate of interest = 10.506%.

(c) Step I: Given rate = 8%

Step II: Frequency = 365 [as it is daily]

Step III: $\dfrac{\text{Rate}}{f} = \dfrac{1\%}{365}$ per month

Step IV: Apply the formula:

$$r_{\text{effective}} = \left[1 + \dfrac{r}{f}\right]^{t \times f} - 1$$

$$= \left[1 + \frac{1}{365 \times 100}\right]^{1 \times 365} - 1$$

= 0.01005

Hence, effective rate of interest = 1.005%.

MORE PROBLEMS ON TIME VALUE OF MONEY

Q1. Indian post-office has launched a product which states that invest a sum of Rs 10,000 today for 10 years and get a sum assured of Rs. 30,000. Find the rate of interest if compounding is:

a) Yearly
b) Monthly
c) Half-yearly
d) Quarterly
e) Daily

Q2. SBI has a deposit scheme having rate of interest of 2% p.a. compounded continuously. Find the effective rate of interest.

Q3. Compare product of SBI & PNB:
SBI: Interest rate of 8% per annum compounded quarterly.
PNB: Interest rate of 10% per annum compounded half-yearly.

Q4. The recurring deposit of Indian post office has a scheme like:
Invest yearly Rs1,000 for 10 years. The rate of interest is 8% per annum.
How much money you will get; if you invest in this scheme?

Q5. You need Rs. 5,000 per year for your personal expenses after retirement i.e. after 30 years. How much you should invest today to get yearly expenses for next 10 years after retirement; if rate of interest is 10% per annum?

Q6. You want to take education loan from OBC Bank. Bank offers you two different options:
Option 1: Rate of interest of 10% compounded half-yearly.

Option 2: Rate of interest of 10% compounded quarterly.
Which option you will select? Other conditions remaining same.

Q7. Investment Manager of Indian post-office has recently proposed a new scheme under MIS scheme of post-office; which is as below:
Invest a particular sum and get 10% rate of interest for infinite life. If you need Rs. 7,000 per year for infinite period; how much you should invest in this scheme?

Q8. Find present values of following Cash Flows:-

Time (years)	0	1	2	3	4	5
Cash Flows	1,000	2,000	3,000	4,000	5,000	6,000

Q9. PC Jewellers; a leading Jewellery company of India has recently launched a program:-
Pay 12 instalments (monthly) and get 2 instalments from PC Jewellers.
[i.e. if you invest Rs. 1,000 per month in this scheme for 12 months; Rs. 2,000 will be given by PC Jewellers and hence, you can do purchase of Rs. 14,000].
Find the rate of interest of the scheme.

Q10. Tanishq, a subsidiary of Titan Industries has launched a scheme; pay 12 instalments (monthly) and get 1 instalment credited in your account by Tanishq. Find the rate of interest of the scheme.

Q11. How much you will receive after 10 years; if you invest:
   a) Rs. 10,000 for 8% rate of interest per annum,
   b) Rs. 10,000 for 8% rate of interest per annum compounded annually.

c) Rs. 10,000 for 8% per annum compounded half-yearly?

Q12. You want to get a sum of Rs. 20 lakh after 20 years. How much you should invest now; if rate of interest is 8% p.a.?

Q13. If you invest in a fixed deposit scheme of PNB which offers 8% per annum. Find the time after which your investment will become:

a) Double
b) Triple
c) 1.5 times
d) 2.5 times
e) 3.5 times
f) 4 times

Q14. In PPF account, Mr. A invests Rs 1,000 every year. How much amount he will get after 30 years if rate of interest is 8% per annum and he invests:

a) At the beginning of the year
b) At the end of the year

Q15. Suppose you want to take car loan of Rs 5 lakh of 5 years duration at 10% per annum compounded monthly. How much is your monthly loan payment?

Q16. You want to take home loan which has a rate of interest of 10% per annum compounded monthly and payable over 10 years. Your loan payment capability per month is Rs. 8,000. How much loan can you take from bank?

Q17. Mr. A has taken personal loan from Indian Bank of Rs. 10

lakh for 10 years at 10% per annum compounded monthly. Find his monthly loan payment amount.

Q18. You are a probationary officer in a bank in loan division. A customer wants to take a personal loan of Rs 5 lakh for 5 years. Rate of interest of this product in your bank is 5% per annum compounded monthly. Find the monthly instalment customer will have to pay.

Q19. Lovely Auto; a subsidiary of a leading business group has a special offer for its employees. This scheme is as:

Employees of Lovely Professional University(LPU) will get a discount of 5% on MRP (Maximum Retail Price)

Mr. Prakash, an employee of LPU has a loan replaying capacity of Rs. 2,000 per month. He wants to borrow for a period of 10 years and rate of interest is 8% per annum compounded monthly. Find:

a) The maximum amount of loan he can borrow under his paying capacity.
b) The maximum MRP of the car; he is eligible for.

Q20. Mr. X invests in PPF (Public Provident Fund) every month an amount of Rs. 1,000. How much he will get after 30 years if rate of interest on PPF is 8.25% per annum compounded monthly?

2 RISK AND RETURN

Risk: Risk is defined as deviation from expected value (return). Deviation can be in positive (upward) as well as negative (downward) direction. Positive deviation is generally in favour of the asset/ portfolio and hence focus is to minimize the negative deviation.

Hence, Risk is defined as the deviation of actual value from expected value.

Return: Return can be classified as:

(i) **Expected Return:** Before investing in any asset, we expect a particular return, known as expected return.

As expect is a probabilistic term and hence, while calculating expected return, we need probability values.

(ii) **Actual Return:** At the time of maturity/ redemption, the return that we actually realized is the "Actual Return".

(iii) **Historical Return:** The return that a particular asset class has given in past. The expected return is calculated by taking the past (historical) return into consideration.

Variance: Variance is the measure of risk associated with any asset's return. It is calculated as the sum of the squared deviation of each possible rate of return from the expected rate of return multiplied by the probability that the rate of return occurs.

$$\text{Variance } (\sigma^2) = \sum p_i [R_i - E(R)]^2 \qquad i = 1 \text{ to } n.$$

$E(R)$ = expected rate of return.

Standard Deviation: is another measure of risk. It is square root of variance.

Type I: Problems based on expected rate of return

Step I: Identify the probability associated with each return given.
Step II: Make a table like:

Probability	Return	Expected Return
P_1	R_1	$P_1 \times R_1$
P_2	R_2	$P_2 \times R_2$
P_3	R_3	$P_3 \times R_3$

Step III: Find the summation of expected return of all possible cases. Like:
$E(R) = P_1 \times R_1 + P_2 \times R_2 + P_3 \times R_3 \ldots\ldots$
$E(R)$ is the expected return taking all conditions into consideration.

Ex1. Suppose you want to buy a share of Reliance Industries Ltd. The probabilities that it will give returns of 10% and 15% are 0.8 and 0.2 respectively. Find the expected rate of return.

Solution:
Step I: Probability of 10% return = 0.8
Probability of 15% return = 0.2

Step II:
Probability	Return	Expected Return
0.8	10%	8%
0.2	15%	3%

Step III: $E(R) = P_1 \times R_1 + P_2 \times R_2 = (8+3)\% = 11\%$
Hence, expected return = 11%

Practice Problems:
Q1. Suppose probability associated with a return of 10% is 0.3 and that of 15% is 0.7. Find the expected rate of return.

Q2. An analyst argues that if economic conditions will be good, India will grow @ 8 %, otherwise @ 5%. The probability that economic conditions will be good is 0.6 and not good is 0.4. Find the expected rate at which India will grow?

Q3. Find expected rate of return if:

Probability	Return
0.3	10%
0.4	6%
0.3	5%

Type II: Problems based on Average Rate of Return

Step I: Take summations of all returns given.
$[R_1+R_2+R_3+\ldots+R_n]$
Step II: Divide the summation calculated by number of periods taken:
$$\bar{R} = [R_1+R_2+R_3+\ldots+R_n]/n$$

Ex1. Suppose you bought a share of ITC Ltd. 10 years back. Returns that you have got in these 10 years are: 8%, 10%, 7%, -7%, -8%, 11%, 20%, 7%, 7%, 10% respectively. Find average rate of return, you have got during entire period.

Solution:
Step I: Summation = [8%+10%+7%-7%-8%+11%+20%+7%+7%+10%] = 65%
Step II: Divide summation by number of periods (i.e. 10).
  Average Return = 65%/10 = 6.5%

Q1. Suppose the return an asset class has given over a period of 5 years are 5 %, 7%, -2%, 10% and 0% respectively. Find average rate of return.

Q2. An asset has given return 50% in 1st year and -50% in 2nd year. Find average rate of return.

Type III: Problems based on standard deviation & variance; when probability values are given.

Step I: Find expected rate of return as shown in type I.
Step II: Make a table like

P_i	R_i	$E(R)$	$R_i - E(R)$	$[R_i - E(R)]^2$	$P_i \times [R_i - E(R)]^2$
P_1	R_1	$E(R)$	$R_1 - E(R)$	$[R_1 - E(R)]^2$	$P_1 \times [R_1 - E(R)]^2$
P_2	R_2	$E(R)$	$R_2 - E(R)$	$[R_2 - E(R)]^2$	$P_2 \times [R_2 - E(R)]^2$

Step III: Take the summation of last column i.e.
$$\sigma^2 = P_1 \times [R_1 - E(R)]^2 + P_2 \times [R_2 - E(R)]^2 + \text{----------}$$
σ^2 is the variance.

Step IV: Take square root i.e
$$\sigma = \sqrt{P_1 \times [R_1 - E(R)]^2 + P_2 \times [R_2 - E(R)]^2 + \text{----------}}$$

Ex1. The probabilities that India will grow @ 10% and 8% are 0.5 and 0.5. Find the variance and standard deviation.

Solution:
Step I: Calculation of expected rate of return.
$$E(R) = P_1 \times R_1 + P_2 \times R_2 = 0.5 \times 10\% + 0.5 \times 8\% = 9\%$$

Step II:

P_i	R_i	$E(R)$	$R_i - E(R)$	$[R_i - E(R)]^2$	$P_i \times [R_i - E(R)]^2$
0.5	10	9	1	1	$0.5 \times 1 = 0.5$
0.5	8	9	1	1	$0.5 \times 1 = 0.5$

Step III:
$$\sigma^2 = 0.5 + 0.5 = 1$$
Hence, variance = 1

Step IV: $\sigma = \sqrt{1} = 1$
Hence, standard deviation = 1.

Q1. Find variance and standard deviation in the following cases:
(i) $P_1 = 0.3$, $P_2 = 0.7$, $R_1 = 8\%$, $R_2 = 7\%$
(ii) $P_1 = 0.2$, $P_2 = 0.3$, $P_3 = 0.5$, $R_1 = 8\%$, $R_2 = 5\%$ and $R_3 = 10\%$.

Q2. You buy stock of a company whose probability of return depends upon weather conditions. If weather will be rainy, you can expect a return of 10%, if normal, return can be 7% and if sunny, return can be 5%. The probabilities that weather will be rainy, normal or sunny are 0.7, 0.2 & 0.1. Find variance and standard deviation of return.

Type IV: Problems based on variance & standard deviation when number of period is given.

Step I: Find average return of period.

$$\overline{R} = [R_1+R_2+R_3+\ldots\ldots\ldots\ldots+R_n]/n$$

Step II: Make a table like:

R_i	$\overline{R}$	$R_i - \overline{R}$	$[R_i - \overline{R}]^2$
R_1	$\overline{R}$	$R_1 - \overline{R}$	$[R_1 - \overline{R}]^2$
R_2	$\overline{R}$	$R_2 - \overline{R}$	$[R_2 - \overline{R}]^2$

Step III: Take summation of last column and divide by (n-1); where n is number of periods.

$$\sigma^2 = [[R_1 - \overline{R}]^2 + [R_2 - \overline{R}]^2 + \text{----------}]/(n-1)$$

This is σ^2 and hence, variance.

Step IV: Take square root of variance; this is standard deviation.

Ex1. Return of an asset over 5 years is given as 5%, 8%, -2%, -5% and 20%. Find variance and standard deviation.

Solution:
Step I: Find average return:

$$\overline{R} = (5+8-2-5+20)/5 = 5.2\%$$

Step II:

R_i	$\overline{R}$	$R_i - \overline{R}$	$[R_i - \overline{R}]^2$
5	5.2	-0.2	0.04
8	5.2	2.8	7.84
-2	5.2	-7.2	51.84
-5	5.2	-10.2	104.04

20	5.2	14.8	219.04

Step III: Summation of last column
$$\sigma^2 = [0.04+7.84+51.84+104.04+219.04]/4 = 95.7$$
Hence, variance = 95.7

Step IV:
Standard Deviation = $\sqrt{\sigma^2}$ = 9.78

Practice Problems

Q1. Find variance and standard deviation in all the following given conditions:
  (i) $R_1 = 5\%$, $R_2 = 7\%$, $R_3 = 8\%$
  (ii) $R_1 = 8\%$, $R_2 = 20\%$, $R_3 = 20\%$, $R_4 = 10\%$
  (iii) $R_1 = 10\%$, $R_2 = 10\%$
  (iv) $R_1 = 10\%$, $R_2 = 5\%$, $R_3 = 7\%$.

In all cases given above, R_i is the return in ith year.

Type V: Problems based on Geometric mean returns (compounded annual rate of return)

Step I: Note returns of all periods given.
Step II: Convert % returns given into decimal points like: 8% = 0.08, 10% =0.1
Step III: Add 1 to each return and multiply them like:
$$(1+0.08) \times (1+0.1) \times \text{------------------}$$
Step IV: Take **n**th root of the product; where n= period of holding.
Step V: Subtract 1 from the outcome of step IV.

Ex1. Suppose share of a company A gives return of 5% and 8% in two years. Find compound annual rate of return as well as holding period return.

Solution:
Step I: Given returns are 5 % and 8%.

Step II: Convert % into decimal as: 5 % = 0.05 and 8% = 0.08
Step III: Add 1 to each returns and multiply i.e.
$$(1.05) \times (1.08) = 1.134$$
Step IV: Here holding period is 2 years hence, square root will be taken of multiplication which is $\sqrt{1.134} = 1.065$

Step V: Subtract 1 i.e. 1.065-1 =0.065 =6.5%.
Hence, compounded annual rate of return = 6.5%.

Holding period return = 1.134-1 = 0.134 = 13.4%
(To calculate holding period return, subtract 1 from outcome of step III).

Practice Problems:
Find compound annual rate of return and holding period return in the following cases:
    (i) $R_1 = 5\%$, $R_2 = -5\%$
    (ii) $R_1 = 2\%$, $R_2 = 8\%$, $R_3 = 7\%$
    (iii) $R_1 = 8\%$, $R_2 = 9\%$ and $R_3 = 10\%$
    (iv) $R_1 = 50\%$ and $R_2 = -20\%$.
              Where R_i is return of ith period.

Solution of Practice Problems

TYPE I:-

Q1. Step I: Probability Associated with 10% return = 0.3

Probability Associated with 15% return = 0.7

Step II:

Probability	Return	Expected Return
0.3	10%	3%
0.7	15%	10.5%

Step III: Expected Return i.e. $E(R) = P_1 \times R_1 + P_2 \times R_2$

= 0.3 x 10% + 0.7 x 15%

= 3% + 10.5% = 13.5%

Hence, Expected Return = 13.5%

Q2. Step I: Probability Associated with 8% return = 0.6

Probability Associated with 5% return = 0.4

Step II:

Probability	Return	Expected Return
0.6	8%	4.8%
0.4	5%	2.0%

Step III: Expected Return i.e. $E(R) = P_1 \times R_1 + P_2 \times R_2$

= 0.6 x 8% + 0.4 x 5%

= 4.8% + 2.0%

= 6.8%

Hence, Expected Rate of growth in India = 6.8%

Q3. **Step I:** No need of this step.

Step II:

Probability	Return	Expected Return
0.3	10%	3%
0.4	6%	2.4%
0.3	5%	1.5%

Step III: Expected Return i.e. $E(R) = P_1 \times R_1 + P_2 \times R_2 + P_3 \times R_3$

$= 0.3 \times 10\% + 0.4 \times 6\% + 0.3 \times 5\%$

$= 3\% + 2.4\% + 1.5\%$

$= 6.9\%$

TYPE II:

Q1. **Step I:** Summation = 5% + 7% - 2% + 10% + 0%

= 20%

Step II: Divide summation by number of periods

= 20% / 5 = 4%

Hence, Average Return = 4% per annum.

Q2. **Step I:** Summation = 50% - 50%

= 0%

Step II: Divide summation by number of periods

= 0% / 2 = 0%

Hence, Average Return = 0% per annum.

TYPE III:

Q1. (i) **Step I:** Calculation of Expected rate of return

$E(R) = (P_1 \times R_1) + (P_2 \times R_2) = (0.3 \times 8\%) + (0.7 \times 7\%)$

= 2.4 % + 4.9% = 7.3%

Step II:

P_i	R_i	$E(R)$	$R_i - E(R)$	$[R_i - E(R)]^2$	$P_i \times [R_i - E(R)]^2$
0.3	8	7.3	0.7	0.49	0.3 × 0.49 = 0.147
0.7	7	7.3	-0.3	0.09	0.7 × 0.09 = 0.063

Step III: $\sigma^2 = 0.147 + 0.063 = 0.21$

Hence, Variance = 0.21

Step IV: Standard Deviation = $\sigma = \sqrt{\sigma^2} = \sqrt{0.21} = 0.458$

(ii). **Step I:** Calculation of Expected rate of return

$E(R) = (P_1 \times R_1) + (P_2 \times R_2) + (P_3 \times R_3)$

$= (0.2 \times 8\%) + (0.3 \times 5\%) + (0.5 \times 10\%) = 8.1\%$

Step II:

P_i	R_i	$E(R)$	$R_i - E(R)$	$[R_i - E(R)]^2$	$P_i \times [R_i - E(R)]^2$
0.2	8	8.1	-0.1	0.01	0.002
0.7	5	8.1	-3.1	9.61	2.883
0.5	10	8.1	-1.9	3.61	1.805

Step III: $\sigma^2 = 0.002 + 2.883 + 1.805 = 4.69$

Hence, Variance = 0.21

Step IV: Standard Deviation = $\sigma = \sqrt{\sigma^2} = \sqrt{4.69} = 2.17$

Q2. **Step I:** Expected Return $E(R) = (P_1 \times R_1) + (P_2 \times R_2) + (P_3 \times R_3)$

$E(R) = (0.7 \times 10\%) + (0.2 \times 7\%) + (0.1 \times 5\%)$

$= 8.9\%$

Step II:

P_i	R_i	$E(R)$	$R_i -$	$[R_i -$	$P_i \times [R_i -$

			E(R)	E(R)]²	E(R)]²
0.7	10	8.9	1.1	1.21	0.847
0.2	7	8.9	-1.9	3.61	0.722
0.1	5	8.9	-3.9	15.21	1.521

Step III: $\sigma^2 = 0.847 + 0.722 + 1.521 = 3.09$

Hence, Variance = 3.09

Step IV: Standard Deviation = $\sigma = \sqrt{\sigma^2} = \sqrt{3.09} = 1.76$

TYPE IV

Q1. (i) **Step I:** Average Return $(\bar{R}) = \dfrac{R_1 + R_2 + R_3}{3}$

$\bar{R} = \dfrac{5 + 7 + 8}{3}\% = 6.67\%$

Step II: Table:

R_i	$\bar{R}$	$R_i - \bar{R}$	$(R_i - \bar{R})^2$
5	6.67	-1.67	2.7889
7	6.67	0.33	0.1089
8	6.67	1.33	1.7689

Step III: Summation of last column

$$\sigma^2 = \frac{1}{2}[2.7889 + 0.1089 + 1.7689] = 2.33$$

Hence, variance = 2.33

Step IV: Standard Deviation = $\sigma = \sqrt{\sigma^2} = \sqrt{2.33} = 1.53$

(ii) **Step I:** Average Return $(\bar{R}) = \dfrac{R_1 + R_2 + R_3 + R_4}{4}$

$$\bar{R} = \frac{8 + 20 + 20 + 10}{4} = 14.5\%$$

Step II: Table:

R_i	$\bar{R}$	$R_i - \bar{R}$	$(R_i - \bar{R})^2$
8	14.5	-6.5	42.25
20	14.5	+5.5	30.25
20	14.5	5.5	30.25
10	14.5	-4.5	20.25

Step III: Summation of last column

$$\sigma^2 = \frac{1}{3}[42.25 + 30.25 + 30.25 + 20.25] = 41$$

Hence, variance = 41

Step IV: Standard Deviation = $\sigma = \sqrt{\sigma^2} = \sqrt{41} = 6.403$

(iii) **Step I:** Average Return $(\bar{R}) = \dfrac{R_1 + R_2}{2}$

$\bar{R} = \dfrac{10 + 10}{2}\% = 10\%$

Step II: Table:

R_i	$\bar{R}$	$R_i - \bar{R}$	$(R_i - \bar{R})^2$
10	10	0	0
10	10	0	0

Step III: Summation of last column

$\sigma^2 = \dfrac{1}{1}[0 + 0] = 0$

Hence, variance = 0

Step IV: Standard Deviation $= \sigma = \sqrt{\sigma^2} = \sqrt{0} = 0$

(iv) **Step I:** Average Return $(\bar{R}) = \dfrac{R_1 + R_2 + R_3}{3}$

$\bar{R} = \dfrac{10 + 5 + 7}{3} = 7.33\%$

Step II: Table:

R_i	$\bar{R}$	$R_i - \bar{R}$	$(R_i - \bar{R})^2$
10	7.33	2.67	7.1289
5	7.33	-2.33	5.4289
7	7.33	-0.33	0.1089

Step III: Summation of last column

$$\sigma^2 = \frac{1}{2}[7.1289 + 5.4289 + 0.1089] = 6.33$$

Hence, variance = 6.33

Step IV: Standard Deviation = $\sigma = \sqrt{\sigma^2} = \sqrt{6.33} = 2.52$

TYPE V

Q1. (i) Step I: Return R_1 = 5 %; R_2 = -5%

Step II: R_1 = 5% = 0.05

R_2 = -5% = -0.05.

Step III: Add 1 to each Return and Multiply i.e.

(1+0.05) x (1-0.05) = 0.9975

Step IV: Here holding period is 2 years and hence, square root will be taken of multiplication which is $\sqrt{0.9975}$ = 0.9987

Step V: Subtract 1 i.e. 0.9987 – 1 = -0.00125 = -0.125%

Hence, Compound Annual rate of return = -0.125%

While, Holding period return = 0.9975 − 1 = −0.0025

= −0.25%

(ii) **Step I**: Return R_1 = 2%; R_2 = 8% & R_3 = 7%

Step II: R_1 = 2% = 0.02

R_2 = 8% = 0.08 & R_3 = 7% = 0.07.

Step III: Add 1 to each return and multiply i.e.

(1+0.02) x (1+0.08) x (1+0.07) = 1.1787

Step IV: Here holding period is 3 years and hence, cube root will be taken of multiplication which is $\sqrt[3]{1.1787}$ = 1.0563

Step V: Subtract 1 i.e. 1.0563 − 1 = 0.0563

= 5.63%

Hence, Compound Annual rate of return = 5.63%

While, Holding period return = 1.1787 − 1 = 0.1787

= 17.87%

(iii) **Step I**: Returns R_1 = 8%; R_2 = 9% & R_3 = 10%

Step II: R_1 = 8% = 0.08

R_2 = 9% = 0.09 & R_3 = 10% = 0.1.

Step III: Add 1 to each return and multiply i.e.

(1+0.08) x (1+0.09) x (1+0.1) = 1.2949

Step IV: Here holding period is 3 years and hence, cube root will be taken of the multiplication i.e., $\sqrt[3]{1.2949} = 1.08996$

Step V: Subtract 1 i.e. $1.08896 - 1 = 0.08996$

$= 8.996\%$

Hence, Compound Annual rate of return = 8.996%

While, Holding period return = $1.2949 - 1 = 0.2949$

$= 29.49\%$

(iv) **Step I**: Returns $R_1 = 50\%$; $R_2 = -20\%$

Step II: $R_1 = 50\% = 0.5$

$R_2 = -20\% = -0.2$

Step III: Add 1 to each return and multiply i.e.

$(1+0.5) \times (1-0.2) = 1.2$

Step IV: Here holding period is 2 years and hence, square root will be taken of the multiplication i.e., $\sqrt{1.2} = 1.0954$

Step V: Subtract 1 i.e. $(1.0954 - 1) = 0.0954$

$= 9.54\%$

Hence, Compound Annual rate of return = 9.54%

While, Holding period return = $1.2 - 1 = 0.2$

$= 20\%$

MORE PROBLEMS ON RISK & RETURN

Q1. Find expected return in following cases:-

	Probability	Return (%)
Case 1	0.7	10%
	0.2	8%
	0.1	2%
Case 2	0.6	10%

		0.4	20%
	⎧	0.7	20%
Case 3	⎨	0.1	30%
	⎩	0.2	15%
	⎧	0.2	10%
Case 4	⎨	0.2	20%
	⎩	0.2	5%
		0.4	30%
	⎧	0.2	10%
	⎪	0.2	20%
Case 5	⎨	0.2	15%
	⎩	0.2	10%
		0.2	8%
	⎧	0.3	20%
Case 6	⎨	0.6	8%
	⎩	0.1	5%
Case 7	⎧	0.2	20%

0.4	8%
0.4	10%

Q2. Subhash will score a return of 8% or 18% if he will on the system for 4 hours and 8 hours respectively in a online trading competition. The probability of being on the system for 4 hours is 0.4 and that of 8 hours is 0.6. Find the expected return Subhash can generate.

Q3. Today SENSEX will entirely depend upon the activity (buying/selling) of FIIs (Foreign Institutional Investors) opined an analyst, The probability of buying and selling by FIIs is 0.3 and 0.7 respectively. SENSEX will generate a return of 10% if buying happens and that of -20% if selling happens. What is the expected return SENSEX will generate today?

Q4. You want to borrow from a bank on floating rate of interest. The current rate of interest is 8%. The probability of interest rate going up (10%) is 0.3 and that of going down is 0.5. The rate of interest if it goes down is 6%. Find the expected rate of interest you will have to pay.

Q5. India is currently facing a problem of rupee depreciation. RBI sees this as a cause of external factors mainly "Euro-zone crisis" and estimates that if "Euro-zone crisis" softens rupee will generate a return of 10%; else -15%. The probability of softening of the crisis is 0.5. Find the expected return that rupee can generate.

Q6. The bond price has an inverse relationship with interest rate. You want to invest in Bonds if expected return is at least 8% p.a. The research you have carried-out shows that Bonds market will generate a return of 10% if interest rate goes down; else a return of 6% p.a. The probability of interest rate going up is 0.2. What will be your decision?

Q7. India is currently facing a problem of high inflation; which is because of high crude oil prices. The inflation will be 10% if crude-oil prices goes up; else 6%. The chance of crude-oil prices going up is 0.7 and that of going down is 0.3. Find the expected inflation India will face.

Q8. You would like to buy shares of NTPC limited, a leading power generating company of India if on an average it has given a return of 10% p.a. For the same, you have collected share prices of NTPC for last 5 years. The returns NTPC Ltd. has given through 2000-2005 (last 5 years) are 8%, 12%, 10%, 15% and -5%. What will be your decision regarding this investment?

Q9. Find Average Rate of Return in following cases:-

	Year	1	2	3	4	5	6	7
(i)	Returns	10%	-10%	-2%	-5%	-6%	-8%	-5%
(ii)	Returns	-10%	2%	3%	7%	12%	8%	5%
(iii)	Returns	-20%	25%	2%	7%	8%	9%	10%
(iv)	Returns	-7%	17%	2%	17%	-9%	-9%	10%
(v)	Returns	10%	0%	-20%	70%	0%	0%	0%
(vi)	Returns	0%	20%	0%	-20%	0%	0%	20%

Q10. The probabilities that Reliance Industries Limited will generate a return of 15% and 10% are 0.3 and 0.7 respectively. Find Expected return, variance and Standard Deviation.

Q11. FDI inflows in a country depends upon its growth @ 5% and 8% are 0.7 and 0.3. Find expected growth rate of Nepal, its standard deviation and variance of growth rate.

Q12. Crop Yield depends mainly on "Rainfall" in Punjab Region, a research report says. The crop yield will be 80% if rainfall is normal; else 30%. The probability of normal rainfall is 0.6 Find expected crop yield, variance and standard deviation of yield.

Q13. Find expected return, variance and standard deviation in following cases:-

(i) $P_1 = 0.3$, $P_2 = 0.4$, $P_3 = 0.3$, $R_1 = 10\%$, $R_2 = 5\%$, $R_3 = 7\%$.

(ii) $P_2 = 0.5$, $P_2 = 0.5$, $R_1 = 20\%$, $R_2 = 80\%$.

(iii) $P_1 = 0.6$, $P_2 = 0.4$, $R_1 = 10\%$, $R_2 = 15\%$.

Q14. Find variance and standard deviation of return of all cases given in question 9.

Q15. Company XYZ Ltd. has given a return of 2%, 7%, -9% and 12% in four consecutive years. Find variance & standard deviation of returns.

Q16. The return and risk data of two financial instruments are given below:

	Risk(Standard Deviation)	Return
Instrument A	20	7%

| Instrument B | 40 | 10% |

Q17. Two similar financial assets having return statistics as given:

Year	1	2	3	4	5
Asset 1	10%	-8%	7%	20%	5%
Asset 2	8%	-7%	15%	8%	5%

Which of the two investment option is a better investment asset for a rational investor?

Q18. Two similar Mutual Funds have given a return as shown:

Year	1	2	3	4
Mutual fund A	10%	-20%	7%	27%
Mutual Fund B	8%	-12%	12%	12%

Which of the two Mutual fund is a better option for a rational investor.

Q19. Two ULIP products, similar in nature, have given following returns:

Year	1	2	3	4	5	6
ULIP 1	10%	8%	7%	12%	18%	-10%

ULIP 2	20%	12%	16%	-27%	10%	-8%

Select the preferred option for

(a) Risk Averse Investors

(b) Risk Seeking Investors

(c) Rational Investors

Q20. Shares of XYZ Ltd. Company has given a return of 8%, 7% and 18% in 3 consecutive years. Find compound annual rate of return as well as Holding period return.

Q21. Find Compound Annual Rate of Return as well as Holding period Return in the following cases:

(a) $R_1 = 8\%$, $R_2 = -10\%$, $R_3 = 25\%$.

(b) $R_2 = 5\%$, $R_2 = 1\%$, $R_3 = 7\%$, $R_4 = 5\%$.

(c) $R_1 = 8\%$, $R_2 = -8\%$

(d) $R_2 = 7\%$, $R_2 = -7\%$, $R_3 = 18\%$

Q22. Being a rational investor; you have to select the best alternative out of given:

Option 1: Probability of 10% return is 0.3 & that of -8% return is 0.8.

Option 2: Probability of 20% return is 0.4 & that of -12% return is 0.6.

Option 3: Probability of 15% return is 0.5 % that of -8% is 0.5.

3 VALUATION OF EQUITY

Objective: To make readers understand the concepts of different approaches of equity valuation.

Valuation: valuation deals with the identification of true value (intrinsic value) of a security.

Broadly, there are two types of price a security can have:-

(a) Intrinsic value:- It is the value an asset can have on the basis of its utility.
(b) Market value :- Market value of an asset is the value (price) reached because of market forces (supply and demand).

Single period valuation Model:

This model assumes that investor holds an equity share for one year only and dividend is paid after 1 year of subscription (purchase). Hence,

$$Po = \frac{D_1}{(1+K_e)} + \frac{P_1}{(1+K_e)}$$

Here, D1 = Expected dividend after 1 year

P1 = Expected price after 1 year.

- This chapter is based on the concept that intrinsic value of an asset is equal to the total cash inflows from that asset discounted to the present value by the expected (required) rate of return.
- If intrinsic value of an asset is higher than its market value asset is under priced (undervalued). Whereas, if intrinsic value of an asset is lower than its market value, asset is overpriced (overvalued).

Multi-period valuation Model:

This model assumes that share is kept for more than one year period.

(a) Finite-period Model

$$Po = \frac{D_1}{(1+K_e)} + \frac{D_2}{(1+K_e)^2} + \cdots + \frac{(D_n + P_n)}{(1+K_e)^n}$$

Where, Di = dividend in ith year.

Pn = price of share in nth year.

(b) Infinite- period Model:

$$Po = \frac{D_1}{(1+K_e)} + \frac{D_2}{(1+K_e)^2} + \frac{D_3}{(1+K_e)^3} \cdots$$

Constant Growth Dividend Discount Model (Gordon Growth Model):

$$Po = \frac{D_0 \times (1+g)}{(K_e - g)} = \frac{D_1}{(K_e - g)}$$

Where, Do = last year dividend

g = dividend growth rate

Ke = cost of equity

D1 = expected dividend this year

When g = 0 (i.e. no growth)

$$Po = \frac{D_0 \times (1+g)}{(K_e - g)} = \frac{D_0}{(K_e)}$$

This model is known as No growth Model.

- Ratio Model :
(i) Book –value Model: Book value per share is defined as the net-worth divide by number of outstanding equity shares.

$$\text{Book value per share} = \frac{NetWorth}{\text{No. of outstanding shares}} = \frac{Equity + Reserves + Surplus}{\text{No. of outstanding shares}}$$

(ii) P/E Model :

Expected P/E is calculated and if the expected P/E is higher than current P/E, share is under-valued.

If E(P/E) < Current P/E → over-priced

and if E(P/E) = Current P/E → correctly priced.

$$\text{Since, P/E} = \frac{\text{Market price}}{\text{Earning per share}}$$

$$\text{Hence, E(P/E)} = \frac{\text{Market price}}{E(EPS)} = \frac{D_1}{K_e - g} \times \frac{1}{E(EPS)}$$

Type I - Problems based on single period model

Step I : Identify expected dividend at the end of the year (D1).

Step II : Identify expected price at the end of the year (P1).

Step III : Identify cost of equity (Ke).

Step IV : Apply the formula :

$$Po = \frac{D_1}{(1+K_e)} + \frac{P_1}{(1+K_e)}$$

Ex1: The expected dividend of Shri Ltd. this year is Rs.5 per share. The expected price of the share at the end of the year is Rs.180. Find the value of the share if the expected rate of return is 10%.

Sol: Step I : Expected dividend (D1) = 5

Step II : Expected price (P1) = 180

Step III : Cost of equity (Ke) = 10%

Step IV : Po = $\dfrac{5}{(1+0.1)} + \dfrac{180}{(1+0.1)}$ = 168.18

Hence, price of the share should be Rs. 168.18.

Note : If share of the Shri Ltd. is trading at Rs. 140 and hence, it is under-valued and must be purchased as its price is expected to rise.

Practice Problems

Q1. The expected dividend of ABC Ltd. at the end of this year is Rs.10, and expected price is Rs.200. Find price of the share if expected rate of return is 15%.

Q2. The expected dividend of ABC Ltd. at the end of this year is Rs.10, and expected price is Rs.300. Find expected rate of return if current price of share is Rs.250.

Q3. The expected dividend of ABC Ltd. at the end of this year is Rs.10, and current share price is Rs.800. Find the expected price at the end of this year of required rate of return is 10%.

Q4. Find whether shares are under-priced, over-priced or correctly priced in the following cases :-

	Expected Dividend at the end of year	Expected price at the end of year	Required rate of return	Current market price
(i)	Rs.8	Rs.200	10	150
(ii)	Rs.7	Rs.300	12%	250
(iii)	Rs.10	Rs.300	12%	250
(iv)	Rs.5	Rs.300	12%	250
(v)	Rs.50	Rs.300	5%	450
(vi)	Rs.2	Rs.100	10%	75
(vii)	Rs.7	Rs.100	10%	75

Type II- Problems based on finite period model

Step I : Identify the expected dividend at the end of each year (D1,D2, ... ,)

Step II : Identify price at the end of the investment period (Pn).

Step III : Identify cost of equity/required rate of return (Ke).

Step IV : Apply the formula :

$$Po = \frac{D_1}{(1+K_e)} + \frac{D_2}{(1+K_e)^2} + - - - + \frac{(D_n + P_n)}{(1+K_e)^n}$$

Ex1: Ramesh wants to buy a share of X Ltd. The investment horizon of Ramesh is 3 years. The expected dividend during the period is Rs.7, Rs.6 and Rs.10. The expected price of share at the end of 3 years is Rs.600 Find the current price of the share if required rate of return is 10%.

Sol: Step I : D1 = 7, D2 = 6, D3 = 10.

Step II : P3 = 600.

Step III : Ke = 10%.

Step IV : $P_o = \dfrac{7}{(1+0.1)} + \dfrac{6}{(1+0.1)^2} + \dfrac{(10+600)}{(1+0.1)^n}$

$\Rightarrow P_o = 469.62$.

Hence, current price of share must be 469.62.

If it is > 469.62, share is over-priced.

Practice Problems

Q1. Mr. A wants to invest in share of company B for 5 years. The expected dividend for 5 years are Rs.5, Rs.10, Rs.15, Rs.20 and Rs.50 respectively. The expected price of share after 5 years is Rs.600. Find current price of share if his expected rate of return is 10%.

Q2. Mr. wants to invest in share of company B for 5 years. The expected dividend for 5 years are Rs.5, Rs.10, Rs.15, Rs.20 and Rs.50 respectively. The current market price of share after 5 years if his required rate of return is 10%.

Q3. Find current price of share if

(a) D1 = 7, D2 = 8, Ke = 5%, P2 = 50.
(b) D2 = (10+i)², Ke = 10%, P4 = 7000, here, i= 1,2,..4.
(c) Di = (2)^i, i = 1 to 3, Ke = 10%, P3 = 70.

Type III – Problems based on consistent growth dividend discount model (Gordon Growth Model) :-

Step I : Identify last year dividend (Do) or Expected dividend this year (D1).

Step II : Identify growth rate (g).

Step III : Identify cost of equity (Ke).

Step IV : Apply the formula :

$$Po = \frac{D_0 \times (1+g)}{(K_e - g)} \quad \text{if Do is given.} \quad \textbf{OR}$$

$$Po = \frac{D_1}{(K_e - g)} \quad \text{if D1 is given.}$$

Ex1: Company X Ltd is expected to grow at the rate of 5% per annum and dividend paid last year was Rs.5 What is the price of share if required rate of return is 10%.

Sol: Step I : Last year dividend (Do) = 5.

Step II : Growth (g) = 5% = 0.05.

Step III : Ke = 10% = 0.1.

Step IV : Po = $\frac{D_0 \times (1+g)}{(K_e - g)}$ → Since Do is given

$$Po = \frac{5 \times (1+0.05)}{(0.1-0.05)} = 105.$$

Practice Problems

Q1. A company is expected to grow at 10% per annum and expected dividend at the end of this year id Rs.100. Find the current price of share if required rate of return is 20%.

Q2. The current price of share of a company as per Gordon growth model is Rs.500. The dividend paid last year is Rs.10 Find the expected growth rate if required rate of return is 20%.

Q3. Find whether shares are over-priced, under-priced or correctly priced in the following cases:-

(a) Do = Rs.10, g = 10% , Ke = 20% Market price of share = 100.
(b) Do = Rs.1, g = 5%, Ke = 7% Market price of share = Rs.200.
(c) Do = Rs.0.5, g = 10%, Ke = 20% Market price of share = Rs.70.
(d) D1 = Rs.20, g = 2%, Ke = 7% Market price of share = Rs.800.
(e) D1 = Rs.2, g = 2%, Ke = 7% Market price of share = Rs.70.
(f) D1 = Rs.7, g = 3%, Ke = 5% Market price of share = Rs.70.
(g) D1=Rs.7, g = 0, Ke = 5% Market price of share = Rs.70.

Solution of Practice Problems

TYPE I:

Q1. Step I: Expected Dividend = Rs. 10

Step II: Expected price = Rs.200

Step III: K_e = 15%

$$P_0 = \frac{D_1}{(1+K_e)} + \frac{P_1}{(1+K_e)}$$

Step IV:

$$= \frac{10}{(1+0.15)} + \frac{200}{(1+0.15)}$$

$$= 182.61$$

Hence, true price of share = 182.61

NOTE: If share price trading in market is higher than 182.61, stock is over-priced; if below 182.61, under-priced.

Q2. Step I: Expected Dividend (D_1) = Rs. 10

Step II: Expected price (P_1) = Rs.300

Step III: K_e = ?

$$P_0 = \frac{D_1}{(1+K_e)} + \frac{P_1}{(1+K_e)}$$

Step IV:

$$250 = \frac{10}{(1+K_e)} + \frac{300}{(1+K_e)}$$

$$250 = \frac{31}{1+K_e}$$

$$\Rightarrow K_e = 0.24 = 24\%$$

Hence, required rate of return = 24%.

Q3. Step I: Expected Dividend (D_1) = Rs. 10

Step II: Expected price (P_1) = ?

Step III: $K_e = 10\%$, P_0 = Rs. 800

$$P_0 = \frac{D_1}{(1+K_e)} + \frac{P_1}{(1+K_e)}$$

Step IV:

$$\Rightarrow 800 = \frac{10}{(1+K_e)} + \frac{P_1}{(1+K_e)}$$

$$\Rightarrow 800 = \frac{10}{(1.10)} + \frac{P_1}{(1.10)}$$

$$\Rightarrow P_1 = 870$$

Hence, expected price = Rs. 870

Q4. (i) Step I: Expected Dividend (D_1) = Rs. 8

Step II: Expected price (P_1) = Rs. 200

Step III: $K_e = 10\%$

$$P_0 = \frac{D_1}{(1+K_e)} + \frac{P_1}{(1+K_e)}$$

Step IV:

$$= \frac{8}{(1+0.10)} + \frac{200}{(1+0.10)}$$

⇨ $P_0 = 189.10$

Hence, correct price of share should be 189.10. As, current market price is Rs.150. Hence, it is under-priced.

(ii) **Step I**: Expected Dividend (D_1) = Rs. 7

Step II: Expected price (P_1) = Rs.300

Step III: $K_e = 12\%$

$$P_0 = \frac{D_1}{(1+K_e)} + \frac{P_1}{(1+K_e)}$$

Step IV:

$$= \frac{7}{(1+0.12)} + \frac{300}{(1+0.12)}$$

⇨ $P_0 = 274.10$

Hence, correct price of share should be 274.10. As, current market price is Rs.250. Hence, it is under-priced.

(iii) **Step I**: Expected Dividend (D_1) = Rs. 10

Step II: Expected price (P_1) = Rs.300

Step III: $K_e = 12\%$

$$P_0 = \frac{D_1}{(1+K_e)} + \frac{P_1}{(1+K_e)}$$

Step IV:

$$= \frac{10}{(1+0.12)} + \frac{300}{(1+0.12)}$$

⇨ $P_0 = 276.79$

Hence, correct price of share should be 276.79 As, current market price is Rs.250. Hence, it is under-valued.

(iv) **Step I**: Expected Dividend (D_1) = Rs. 5

Step II: Expected price (P_1) = Rs.300

Step III: K_e = 12%

$$P_0 = \frac{D_1}{(1+K_e)} + \frac{P_1}{(1+K_e)}$$

Step IV:

$$= \frac{5}{(1+0.12)} + \frac{300}{(1+0.12)}$$

⇨ P_0 = 272.32

As, current market price is Rs.250 which is less than Rs. 272.32 and hence stock is under-priced.

(v) **Step I**: Expected Dividend (D_1) = Rs. 50

Step II: Expected price (P_1) = Rs.300

Step III: K_e = 5%

$$P_0 = \frac{D_1}{(1+K_e)} + \frac{P_1}{(1+K_e)}$$

Step IV:

$$= \frac{50}{(1+0.05)} + \frac{300}{(1+0.05)}$$

⇨ P_0 = 333.33

Hence, correct price of share should be Rs. 333.33. As, market price is Rs.450. Therefore, stock is over-priced.

(vi) **Step I**: Expected Dividend (D_1) = Rs. 2.0

Step II: Expected price (P_1) = Rs. 100

Step III: $K_e = 10\%$

$$P_0 = \frac{D_1}{(1+K_e)} + \frac{P_1}{(1+K_e)}$$

Step IV:

$$= \frac{2}{(1+0.1)} + \frac{100}{(1+0.1)}$$

$\Rightarrow P_0 = 92.73$

Hence, correct price of share = Rs. 92.73. As, stock is trading at Rs. 75; hence, it is under-priced.

(vii) **Step I**: Expected Dividend (D_1) = Rs. 7

Step II: Expected price (P_1) = Rs. 100

Step III: $K_e = 10\%$

$$P_0 = \frac{D_1}{(1+K_e)} + \frac{P_1}{(1+K_e)}$$

Step IV:

$$= \frac{7}{(1+0.1)} + \frac{100}{(1+0.1)}$$

$\Rightarrow P_0 = 92.27$

As stock is trading at Rs. 75 and hence, stock is under-priced.

TYPE II

Q1. **Step I**: $D_1 = 5$, $D_2 = 10$, $D_3 = 15$, $D_4 = 20$, $D_5 = 50$

Step II: Price at the end of 5th year $P_5 = 600$

Step III: $K_e = 10\%$

Step IV:

$$P_0 = \frac{D_1}{(1+K_e)} + \frac{D_2}{(1+K_e)^2} + \frac{D_3}{(1+K_e)^3} + \frac{D_4}{(1+K_e)^4} + \frac{D_5+P_5}{(1+K_e)^5}$$

$$P_0 = \frac{5}{(1+0.1)} + \frac{10}{(1+0.1)^2} + \frac{15}{(1+0.1)^3} + \frac{20}{(1+0.1)^4} + \frac{50+600}{(1+0.1)^5}$$

⇨ $P_0 = 441.34$

Hence, correct price of share should be Rs. 441.34.
If Market price > 441.34 ⇨ over-valued.
Market price < 441.34 ⇨ under-valued.
Market price = 441.34 ⇨ correctly valued.

Q2. Step I: $D_1 = 5$, $D_2 = 10$, $D_3 = 15$, $D_4 = 20$, $D_5 = 50$

Step II: Price at the end of 5th year $P_5 = ?$

Step III: $K_e = 10\%$

Step IV:

$$P_0 = \frac{D_1}{(1+K_e)} + \frac{D_2}{(1+K_e)^2} + \frac{D_3}{(1+K_e)^3} + \frac{D_4}{(1+K_e)^4} + \frac{D_5+P_5}{(1+K_e)^5}$$

$$300 = \frac{5}{(1+0.1)} + \frac{10}{(1+0.1)^2} + \frac{15}{(1+0.1)^3} + \frac{20}{(1+0.1)^4} + \frac{50+P_5}{(1+0.1)^5}$$

$$\Rightarrow 300 = 37.74 + \frac{50 + P_5}{(1 + 0.1)^5}$$

$$\Rightarrow 50 + P_5 = 422.37$$

$$\Rightarrow P_5 = 372.37$$

Hence, expected price of share after 5 years = Rs.372.37.

Q3. (a) **Step I**: $D_1 = 7$, $D_2 = 8$

Step II: $P_2 = 50$

Step III: $K_e = 5\%$

Step IV:
$$P_0 = \frac{D_1}{(1+K_e)} + \frac{D_2 + P_2}{(1+K_e)^2}$$

$$\frac{7}{(1+0.05)} + \frac{50+8}{(1+0.05)^2}$$

$$\Rightarrow P_0 =$$
$$\Rightarrow P_0 = Rs\ 59.27$$

Hence, current price of share = Rs.59.27.

(b) **Step I**: $D_i = (10 + i)^2$, $i = 1, 2, 3, 4$.

$D_1 = (10 + 1)^2 = 121$, $D_2 = (10 + 2)^2 = 144$,

$D_3 = (10 + 3)^2 = 169$, $D_4 = (10 + 4)^2 = 196$.

Step II: $P_4 = 7000$

Step III: $K_e = 10\%$

Step IV:

$$P_0 = \frac{D_1}{(1+K_e)} + \frac{D_2}{(1+K_e)^2} + \frac{D_3}{(1+K_e)^3} + \frac{D_4+P_4}{(1+K_e)^4}$$

$$P_0 = \frac{121}{(1+0.1)} + \frac{144}{(1+0.1)^2} + \frac{169}{(1+0.1)^3} + \frac{196+7000}{(1+0.1)^4}$$

$\Rightarrow P_0 = 5270.95$

Hence, correct price of share = Rs.5270.95 .

(c) **Step I**: $D_i = (2)^i$, $i = 1, 2, 3$.

$D_1 = (2)^1 = 2$, $D_2 = (2)^2 = 4$, $D_3 = (2)^3 = 8$

Step II: $P_3 = 70$

Step III: $K_e = 10\%$

Step IV:

$$P_0 = \frac{D_1}{(1+K_e)} + \frac{D_2}{(1+K_e)^2} + \frac{D_3+P_3}{(1+K_e)^3}$$

$$= \frac{2}{(1+0.1)} + \frac{4}{(1+0.1)^2} + \frac{8+70}{(1+0.1)^3}$$

$\Rightarrow P_0 =$
$\Rightarrow P_0 = 63.73$

Hence, current price of share should be Rs.63.73 .

TYPE III

Q1. **Step I**: Expected Dividend D_1 = Rs. 100

Step II: g = 10% = 0.1

Step III: $K_e = 0.2$ i.e, 20%

$$P_0 = \frac{D_1}{(K_e - g)} = \frac{100}{0.2 - 0.1} = 1000$$

Step IV:

Hence, current price of share = Rs. 1000.

Q2. Step I: Dividend paid D_0 = Rs. 10

Step II: g = ?

Step III: K_e = 20% = 0.2 , P_0 = 500

$$P_0 = \frac{D_0(1+g)}{(K_e - g)} = \frac{10(1+g)}{0.2 - g}$$

Step IV:

⇨ $500 = \dfrac{10(1+g)}{0.2 - g}$

⇨ $100 - 500g = 10(1+g)$

⇨ $90 = 510g$

⇨ $g = 17.65\%$

Hence, growth rate = 17.65%.

Q3. (a) Step I: D_0 = Rs. 10

Step II: g = 10% = 0.1

Step III: K_e = 20% = 0.2

$$P_0 = \frac{D_0(1+g)}{(K_e - g)} = \frac{10(1+0.1)}{0.2 - 0.1} = 110$$

Step IV:

Hence, true value of share should be Rs. 110. Since, market price is Rs. 100 and hence, share is under-priced and hence, we should buy it.

(b) **Step I:** $D_0 = $ Rs. 1

Step II: $g = 5\% = 0.05$

Step III: $K_e = 7\% = 0.07$

$$P_0 = \frac{D_0(1+g)}{(K_e - g)} = \frac{1(1+0.05)}{0.07 - 0.05} = 52.5$$

Step IV:

Hence, current price of share = Rs.52.50. As, current market price is Rs.200 and hence, stock is over-priced and therefore we should avoid it. The alternative strategy can be to sell (short) it.

(c) **Step I:** $D_0 = 0.5$

Step II: $g = 10\% = 0.1$

Step III: $K_e = 20\% = 0.2$

$$P_0 = \frac{D_0(1+g)}{(K_e - g)} = \frac{0.5(1+0.1)}{0.2 - 0.1} = 5.5$$

Step IV:

Hence, correct price of share = Rs.5.50. As the market price is Rs.70, hence, stock is over-priced. Therefore, it should be avoided. The alternative strategy could be "short" it.

(d) **Step I:** $D_0 = 20$

Step II: g = 2% = 0.02

Step III: K_e = 7% = 0.07

$$P_0 = \frac{D_0}{(K_e - g)} = \frac{20}{0.07 - 0.02} = 400$$

Step IV:

Hence, correct price of share = Rs.400. As the share is trading at Rs.800, hence, it is over-priced.

(e) **Step I:** D_0 = 2

Step II: g = 2% = 0.02

Step III: K_e = 7% = 0.07

$$P_0 = \frac{D_0}{(K_e - g)} = \frac{2}{0.07 - 0.02} = 40$$

Step IV:

Hence, correct price of share = Rs 40. As the share is trading at Rs.70; hence, it is over-priced.

(f) **Step I:** D_1 = 7

Step II: g = 3% = 0.03

Step III: K_e = 5% = 0.05

$$P_0 = \frac{D_1}{(K_e - g)} = \frac{7}{0.05 - 0.03} = 350$$

Step IV:

Hence, correct price of share = Rs.350. As the share is trading at Rs.70; hence, it is under-priced. Thus, we should buy it.

(g) **Step I**: $D_1 = 7$

Step II: $g = 0$

Step III: $K_e = 5\% = 0.05$

$$P_0 = \frac{D_1}{(K_e - g)} = \frac{7}{0.05 - 0} = 140$$

Step IV:

Hence, correct price of share = Rs.140. As the share is trading at Rs.70; hence, it is under-priced. Therefore, we should buy it.

MORE PROBLEMS ON VALUATION OF EQUITY

Q1. A company has a book – value per share of Rs.137.80. Its return on equity is 15% and follows a policy of retaining 60% of its annual earnings. If the opportunity cost of capital is 18%, what is the price of its share? Use perpetual growth model.

[C.A. (Final) Nov. 2011]

Q2. Shares of Voyage Ltd. are being quoted at a price – earning ratio of 8 times. The company retains 45% of its earnings which are Rs.5 per share. Calculate:

(a) The cost of equity to the company if the market expects a growth rate of 15% p.a.
(b) If the anticipated growth rate is 16% p.a., calculate the indicative price with the same cost of capital.
(c) If the company's cost of capital is 20% p.a.; and the anticipated growth rate is 19% p.a.; Calculate the market price per share.

[C.A.(Final) May, 2011]

Q3. The following information is given for QB Ltd.
Earnings per share   Rs. 12
Dividend per share   Rs. 3
Cost of capital   18%
Internal rate of return on investment   22%
Retention ratio   40%
Calculate the market price of share using:
(a) Gordon's Formula   (b) Walter's Formula

[C.A.(Final) May, 2011]

Q4. The expected dividends of XY ltd. for next three years are Rs.10, Rs.20 and Rs.30 respectively. The expected price of share at the end of third year is Rs.67. Find the market price of share if required rate of return is 15%.

Q5. Three companies of power sector repeat its dividend policy after every 3 years. The dividends paid in last 1, 2 and 3 year are Rs.70, Rs.60 and Rs.80. This year onwards also, company is expected to follow the same strategy. Find the best option an investor has on the basis of given information:

Company	Current market price	Market price after 3 years
A	800	270
B	600	320
C	200	25

Q6. Dividend paid by company Book ltd. last year is Rs.70. The expected growth rate of dividend is 10% forever. Find the cost of equity; if current market price is Rs.700.

Q7. Suggest whether the stocks are over-valued, under-valued or correctly priced:

(a) Dividend paid last year D_0 = Rs.10
Expected growth rate of dividend = 8%
Cost of equity = 15%
Current market price of share = Rs.33

(b) Dividend paid over last 3 years = Rs.10, Rs.15 and Rs.20
Cost of equity = 25%
Current market price of share = Rs.80

(c) Dividend paid over last 4 years = Rs.10, Rs.15, Rs.20 and Rs.40

Cost of equity = 21%
Current market price of share = Rs.800

(d) Expected dividend for next 2 years = Rs.10 and Rs.20
Cost of equity = 32%
Current market price of share = Rs.530

(e) $D_1 = 50$, $P_0 = 700$, $K_e = 20\%$, $g = 12\%$.
[Use constant growth model in all cases.]

Q8. Find expected price of share at the end of 5th year if:

(a) $D_1 = Rs.2$, $D_2 = Rs.10$, $D_3 = Rs.20$, $D_4 = Rs.25$, $D_5 = Rs.20$. $P_0 = Rs.100$ and cost of equity = 10%.
(b) $D_i = \sqrt[i]{20}$, $P_0 = Rs.200$, Cost of equity = 20%.
(c) $D_i = (2 + i)^i$, $P_0 = Rs. 1000$, Cost of equity = 15%
(d) $D_i = (3)^i$, $P_0 = Rs. 300$, Cost of equity = 20%
(e) $D_i = (7 - i)^i$, $P_0 = Rs. 3000$, Cost of equity = 20%

Q9. A company pays a constant dividend of Rs.30 every year. Find the current market price if the required rate of return is 15%.

Q10. A researcher would like to verify the relationship of market price of equity with required rate of return. Based on the given data; what will be the conclusion of researcher:

Market price	Required Rate of Return
300	15%
400	11.25%

200	22.50%
150	30%
450	10%

[Use Zero Growth Model].

Q11. Company X Ltd. has a book value of Rs.100 per share. Its return on equity is 18% and follows a policy of dividend pay-out of 30%. Find the price of share if required rate of return is 20%. [Use Gordon Model].

Q12. Company AB Ltd. has a book – value of Rs.700 per share. Its return on equity is 15% and following a retention policy of 80%. Find the price of share if:
   (a) Required rate of return is 15%.
   (b) Required rate of return is 18%.   [Use Gordon Model].

Q13. The expected dividend at the end of this year is Rs.30. The growth rate is 12%. If current price of share is Rs.300, find required rate of return.

Q14. A company has paid Rs.5, Rs.7, Rs.9, Rs.11 and Rs.13 as dividend over last five years and is expected to follow the same growth rate. Find:

   (a) Price of share; if required rate of return = 10%.
   (b) Required rate of return; if price of share is Rs.800.
   (c) Price of share; if required rate of return = 15%.
   (d) Required rate of return; if price of share is Rs.100.

Q15. Find the price of the share if company had paid a dividend of Rs.80 this year and the growth rate is 10%. Required rate of return is 20%.

4 VALUATION OF BONDS

Objective : To enable readers to understand the concepts of bonds, identification of its intrinsic features and valuation of bonds.

Face Value : Face value is the value written on the bond certificate. It is also known as par value.

Coupon Rate : Generally bonds pay a regular interest (at a certain frequency) to its investors. This is a particular % of face value, known as coupon rate.

Market Value : The value at which the bond is trading in markets. This market value can be more or less than the face value.

→ If Market value > Face value, we say bond is trading at premium.
→ If Market value < Face value, we say bond is trading at discount.

Current yield : Current yield is the ratio coupon to current market price.

$$\text{Current yield} = \frac{Coupon}{Current Market\ Price}$$

Yield-to-maturity : This is the rate of return that will be generated if the bond is held till maturity, i.e. it gives internal rate of return of bond.

YTM depends upon the interest rate prevailing in the market.

Redemption value : This is the value that investor will get on the date of maturity. It can be more than face value (at premium); can be at par (face value) or can be at a discount (less than face value). But, generally redemption is done on face value.

Type I- Problems based on coupon payments.

Step I : Identify the face value.

Step II : Identify coupon rate.

Step III : Find coupon by multiplying the coupon rate with face value.

i.e. Coupon (c) = Face value * Coupon rate.

Step IV : Identify frequency of payment.

Step V : Write flow as –

    Time (years) t : 0   1   2   3   4 …….

    Coupon   C C C C C…..

Ex1 : Write the coupon flow statement for a bond of face value Rs.100 and coupon rate 10%annually.

Sol : Step I : Face value (F) = Rs.100

    Step II : Coupon Rate = 10%

    Step III : Coupon (c) = face value * coupon rate

                = 100*10%

                = 10.

Step IV : Frequency = annual

Step V : time (years)   1   2   3   4   5 …..

   Coupon   10 10 10 10 10

Ex2 : Write the coupon flow statement for a bond of face value Rs.100 and coupon rate 10% payable semi-annually.

Sol : Step I : Face Value (F) = Rs.100

   Step II : Coupon rate = 10% = 5% annually

   Step III : Coupon (c) = Face value * coupon rate

        = 1000*10%

        = 100 annually = 50 semi-annually

   Step IV : Frequency = Semi-annually.

   Step V : Coupon flow :

      Time (years)   ½   1 $1^{1/2}$ 2 $2^{1/2}$ 3

      Coupon   50 50 50 50 50 50

Note : As discussed in Chapter 1 (Time value of Money); as frequency has become twice (semi-annually) and hence coupon payment will become half and time period twice.

i.e. Divide coupon rate by frequency (c/f).

& Multiply Time with frequency.

In the problem given above;

Coupon = 100, f = 2 and hence,

Semi-annual coupon = c/f = 100/2 = 50.

Time = 1 year = 2 semi-annual.

Ex3 : Write the coupon flow statement for a bond of face value Rs.100 and coupon rate 5%   payable quarterly.

Sol : Step I : Face value (F) = Rs.100

   Step II : Coupon rate = 5%

   Step III : Coupon = F * coupon rate

       = 100 * 5% = 5 (annual)

   Hence, coupon quarterly = 4 times a year.

   Step V : Coupon flow :

       Time (years)   ¼   2/4   ¾   1 ......

       Coupon   1.25 1.25 1.25 1.25   →Rs 5 (annual coupon)

Practice Problems

Q1. Write the coupon flow statement of a bond of face value Rs.1000, coupon rate 5%, payable annually.

Q2. Write coupon payment statement of the following for one year only.

	Face value	Coupon rate	frequency
i.	100	8%	annually
ii.	100	8%	semi-annually

| iii. | 100 | 8% | quarterly |
| iv. | 100 | 8% | monthly. |

Type II - Problems based on Cash Flows

Step I : Identify face value, coupon rate and market price.

Step II : Calculate Coupon.

Step III : Identify frequency and take required adjustments as stated in Type I.

Step IV : Write cash flow as –

    Time (years) 0 1 2 3 4

    Cash flow   C C C C [C + face value]

Note : At the end of 4th year (at maturity); coupon + maturity value (i.e. face value) both will be paid. ( ) → -ve cash flow (i.e. cash outflow).

Ex1 : Write a cash flow statement of a bond having face value Rs.100, coupon rate 10%, time to maturity 2 years, market price Rs.80, interest payable annually.

Sol : Step I : Face value = Rs.100, coupon rate 10%, time to maturity 2 years, market price Rs.80, interest payable annually.

    Step II : Coupon = Rs.10

    Step III : frequency = Annuity

    Step IV : Cash flows –

Time (years)   0   1   2

Cash flow   -80 10 10+100 ——— redemption value
                  /
            Market price

Ex.2 : Write a cash flow statement of a bond having face value Rs.1000, coupon rate 10%, time to maturity 3 years and market price Rs.800. Interest (coupon) payable semi-annually.

Sol : Step I : Face value = 1000, coupon rate 10%, time to maturity 3 years and market price Rs.800. Interest (coupon) payable semi-annually.

Hence, coupon = 1000 * 10/100 = 100.

   Step II : Coupon = 100.

   Step III : frequency = semi-annual, Hence, coupon = c/f = 100/2 = 50.

   Step IV : Cash flow –

   Time (years)   0   ½   1 $1^{1/2}$ 2 $2^{1/2}$ 3

   Cash flow   -800 50 50 50   50   50   50+1000

                  ↓   ↓
            Purchase price   Redemption value

Practice Problem

Q1. Write the cash flow statements of bonds having following features :

	Face value	Coupon rate	frequency	Time to maturity
i.	100	10%	annually	3 years
ii.	100	8%	annually	2 years
iii.	1000	8%	semi-annually	2 years
iv.	1000	10%	quarterly	2 years
v.	1000	8%	monthly	1 year
vi.	100	8%	semi-annually	2 years.

Market value in all the above cases is 90% of face value [i.e. if face value is 100, market value is 90 & if face value is 1000, market value is 900].

Type III-Problems based on Current yield

Step I : Find face value , coupon rate and calculate coupon.

Step II : Identity current market price.

Step III : Apply formula –

$$\text{Coupon yield} = \frac{Annual Coupon}{Current Market \operatorname{Pr}ice}$$

Ex1 : Find the current yield of a bond having face value Rs.100, coupon rate = 10% annual, current market price of bond = Rs.80.

Sol : Step I : Face value = Rs.100, coupon rate = 10% annual, current market price of bond = Rs.80.

Step II : Current yield = $\dfrac{Annual Coupon}{Current Market Price}$

Step III : Hence,

Current yield = 10/80 = 0.125

= 1.25%

Note : In both cases, current yield is 1.25%. Since , we take annual coupon to calculate current yield and hence, no need to do any adjustment.

Practice Problems

Q1. Find current yield in the following cases –

	Face value	Coupon rate	frequency	Current market price
i.	100	8%	annual	80
ii.	100	8%	semi-annual	80
iii.	100	8%	quarterly	80
iv.	100	10%	annual	90
v.	100	10%	annual	110
vi.	1000	8%	semi-annual	1100.

Type IV - Problems based on calculation of YTM

Step I : Identify face value, coupon rate.

Hence, calculate coupon.

Step II : Apply the formula –

$$\text{Market price (P)} = \frac{C}{(1+r)} + \frac{C}{(1+r)^2} + - - - - - + \frac{C+F}{(1+r)^n}$$

n = Time to maturity, C = Coupon, r = YTM, F = Face value.

By trial and error method, find r i.e. YTM.

An alternative approach to calculate YTM is directly apply the formula to get an approx..idea.

$$\text{YTM} = \frac{C + (F-P)/n}{(0.4 \times F + 0.6 \times P)}$$

F = face value, P = market price, C = annual coupon

n = time to maturity.

Ex1 : Find YTM of a bond having face value Rs.100, coupon rate 10% per annum and current market price Rs.110 and term to maturity 2 years.

Sol : Step I : Face value = Rs.100, coupon rate = 10% per annum and current market price = Rs.110 and term to maturity = 2 years.

Step II : Formula –

$$110 = \frac{10}{(1+r)} + \frac{10+100}{(1+r)^2}$$

r = 0.0465   or   - 1.955

= 4.65%   or   - 195.5%

Rejecting r = − 195.5%

Hence, r = 4.65% (YTM).

Alternatively, for calculation purpose only, if we could have applied formula :

$$\text{YTM} = \frac{C + (F-P)/n}{(0.4 \times F + 0.6 \times P)} = \frac{10 + (100-110)/2}{(0.4 \times 100 + 0.6 \times 110)}$$

= 0.0472 = 4.72%.

Which is almost equal to 4.65%.

Ex2 : Find YTM of a bond having a face value Rs. 100, coupon rate 10% payable semi-annually and current market price of bond Rs.80, time to maturity 2 years.

Sol : Step I : Face value = Rs.100, coupon rate = 10% payable semi-annually and current market price of bond = Rs.80, time to maturity = 2 years.

Step II : Formula –

$$80 = \frac{5}{(1+r)^{0.5}} + \frac{5}{(1+r)^1} + \frac{5}{(1+r)^{1.5}} + \frac{5+100}{(1+r)^2}$$

r = 24.5%

Using short-cut formula, YTM = 22.72%.

Practice Problem

Q1. Calculate YTM of bonds having following features :

Face value Coupon rate frequency Time to maturity Market price

(i) 100	8%	annual	2		90
(ii) 100	8%	annual	2		115
(iii) 100	5%	annual	1		100
(iv) 100	8%	semi-annual	1	80	
(v) 100	8%	quarterly	1	95	
(vi) 100	10%	monthly	1	90.	

Type V – Problems based on bond valuation

Step I : Identify face value, coupon rate. Calculate coupon.

Step II : Identify market price of bond & required rate of return / interest rate prevailing in the market.

Step III : Apply the formula –

$$\text{Price (P) calculated} = \frac{C}{(1+r)} + \frac{C}{(1+r)^2} + \cdots + \frac{C+F}{(1+r)^n}$$

Step IV : If $P_{calculated}$ > Market price, Bond is under-valued &

if $P_{calculated}$ < Market price, Bond is over-valued

if $P_{calculated}$ = Market price, Bond is correctly priced.

Ex1 : A bond having a face value of Rs.100, coupon rate 8% annually and term to maturity 2 years is trading at Rs.80. Find whether the bond is trading at under-valued, over-valued or correctly valued; if required rate of return = 10%.

Sol : Step I : Face value = Rs.100, coupon rate = 8% annually

Hence, Coupon = 100*8/100 = Rs.8

$$\text{Step II}: P_{calculated} = \frac{8}{(1+0.10)} + \frac{8+100}{(1+0.10)^2}$$

$$= 96.53.$$

Step IV : Since,

$P_{calculated} >$ Market price and

Hence, Bond is under-valued.

Practice Problems

Q1. Check whether the bonds given below is under-valued, over-valued or correctly valued :-

S.No.	Face Value($)	Coupon Rate	Time to Maturity (Year)	Market Price ($)	Required Rate of Return
i	100	10%	2	90	8%
ii	100	8%	2	97	8%
iii	100	10%	3	99	7%
iv	100	10%	4	100	10%
v	100	7%	3	90	8%
vi	100	8%	2	110	12%
vii	100	10%	2	110	12%

Type VI – Problems based on valuation of Convertible Bonds.

Step I : Identify face value, coupon rate. Hence, calculate coupon (c).

Step II : Identify conversion ratio and price of equity share on conversion (P_e).

Step III : Identify required rate of return (r) and years to maturity (n).

Step IV : Apply the formula –

Price(P) =

$$\frac{C}{(1+r)} + \frac{C}{(1+r)^2} + - - - - - + \frac{C + P_e \times ConversionRatio}{(1+r)^n}$$

Ex1 : Company XYZ Ltd. has issued a convertible bond at a face value of Rs.1000, having coupon rate of 10% per annum which is convertible to 20 equity shares at the end of 2 years. The expected price of equity shares on conversion i.e. at the end of 2 years is Rs.60. Find the value of convertible bond, if required rate of return is 8%.

Sol : Step I : Face value (F) = 100, Coupon rate = 10%

Hence, Coupon = 100   [1000*10/100]

Step II : Conversion ratio = 20 equity shares; Price of each share (P_e) = 60.

Step III : Required rate of return (r) = 8.1%, n = 2 years

Step IV : Price (P) = 100/(1+0.08) + 20*60 +100/(1+0.08)

i.e. P = 1207.40

Hence, correct price of convertible bond = Rs.1207.40.

If it is issued at a price less than Rs.1207.40, it is under-valued and hence, we should subscribe.

If subscribed at a price higher than Rs.1207.40, it is over-valued and hence should be avoided.

Practice Problems

Q1. Identify the value of convertible bonds in all the following cases –

S.N.	Face Value ($)	Coupon Rate (%)	Conversion Ratio	Price Per Share on Conversion ($)	Time to Maturity	Required Return
i	100	10%	15	5	2	8%
ii	100	10%	10	8	2	7%
iii	1000	5%	20	40	3	10%
iv	1000	15%	15	50	3	12%
v	500	10%	20	20	4	8%
vi	500	8%	20	22	1	14%
vii	400	10%	20	30	2	15%
viii	400	8%	20	10	1	20%

SOLUTION OF PRACTICE PROBLEMS

TYPE I

Q1. Step I: Face value (F) = Rs. 1000

Step II: Coupon Rate = 5%

Step III: Coupon = Face Value X Coupon Rate

= 1000 X 5/100

= 50 (annual)

Step IV: Coupon flow:

Time (years)   1   2   3 ……….till maturity
Coupon   50 50 50………

Q2. (i) Step I: Face value (F) = Rs. 100

Step II: Coupon Rate = 8%

Step III: Coupon = Face Value X Coupon Rate

= 100 X 8/100

= 8

Step IV: Coupon flow:

Time (years)   1
Coupon   8

(ii) Step I: Face value (F) = Rs. 100

Step II: Coupon Rate = 8%

Step III: Coupon = Face Value X Coupon Rate

= 100 X 8/100

= 8 (annual)

Hence, coupon semi-annually = C/f = 8/2 = 4.

Step IV: Frequency = 2 times a year.

Step V: Coupon flow:

Time (years)   ½   1
Coupon (Rs.)   4   4

(iii) **Step I**: Face value (F) = Rs. 100

Step II: Coupon Rate = 8%

Step III: Coupon = Face Value X Coupon Rate

= 100 X 8/100

= 8

Hence, quarterly coupon = C/f = 8/4 = 2.

Step IV: Frequency = 4 times a year.

Step V: Coupon flow:

Time (years)   ¼   2/4   ¾   4/4
Coupon (Rs.)   2   2   2   2

(iv) **Step I**: Face value (F) = Rs. 100

Step II: Coupon Rate = 8%

Step III: Coupon = Face Value X Coupon Rate

= 100 X 8/100

= 8 (annual)

Hence, monthly coupon = C/f = 8/12 = 2/3.

Step IV: Frequency = Monthly

Step V: Coupon flow:

Time (years) 1/12 2/12 3/12 4/12 .... 12/12

Coupon (Rs.) 2/3 2/3 2/3 2/3 .... 2/3

TYPE II

Q1. (i) **Step I:** Face value (F) = Rs. 100, Coupon Rate = 10%,

Market price = 90% of face value = 90 x 100/100 = 90

Step II: Coupon = Face Value x Coupon rate
= 100 x 10/100 = 10 (annual)

Step III: Frequency = Annual

Step V: Cash - flow:

Time (years) 0   1   2   3

Cash flow (Rs.)   -90 10   10   10+100

(ii) **Step I:** Face value (F) = Rs. 100, Coupon Rate = 8%,

Market price = 90% of face value = 90 x 100/100 = 90

Step II: Coupon = Face Value x Coupon rate
= 100 x 8/100 = 8 (annual)

Step III: Frequency = Annual

Step IV: Cash - flow:

Time (years) 0   1   2

Cash flow (Rs.)   -90 8   8+100

(iii) **Step I:** Face value (F) = Rs. 1000, Coupon Rate = 8%,

Market price = 1000 x 90/100 = 900

Step II: Coupon = Face Value x Coupon rate
= 1000 x 8/100 = 80 (annual)
Step III: Coupon at Frequency = C/f = 80/2 = 40 (semi-annual)
Step IV: Frequency = Semi - annually
Step V: Cash - flow:

Time (years)	0	½	2/2	3/2	4/2
Cash flow (Rs.)	-900	40	40	40	40+1000

(iv) **Step I**: Face value (F) = Rs. 1000, Coupon Rate = 10%,

Market price = 1000 x 90/100 = 900

Step II: Coupon = Face Value x Coupon rate
= 1000 x 10/100 = 100
Step III: Coupon at Frequency = C/f = 100/4 = 25
Step IV: Frequency = Quarterly
Step V: Cash - flow:

Time (years)	0	¼	2/4	¾	4/4	5/4	…….	8/4
Cash flow (Rs.)	-900	25	25	25	25	25		25+1000

(v) **Step I**: Face value (F) = Rs. 1000, Coupon Rate = 8%,

Market price = 1000 x 90/100 = 900

Step II: Coupon = Face Value x Coupon rate
= 1000 x 8/100 = 80 (annual)

Step III: Coupon at Frequency = C/f = 80/12 = 6.67

Step IV: Frequency = Monthly

Step V: Cash - flow:

Time (years)   0   1/12   2/12   3/12   .... 12/12
Cash flow (Rs.) -900   6.67   6.67   6.67 ...... 6.67+1000

(vi) **Step I:** Face value (F) = Rs. 100, Coupon Rate = 8%,

Market price = 100 x 90/100 = 90

Step II: Coupon = Face Value x Coupon rate
= 100 x 8/100 = 8 (annual)
Hence, semi-annual coupon = 8/2 = 4.

Step III: Coupon at Frequency = C/f = 8/2 = 4

Step IV: Frequency = Semi-annual

Step V: Cash - flow:

Time (years)   0   1/2   2/2   3/2   4/2
Cash flow (Rs.) -90   4   4   4   4+100

TYPE III:

Q1. (i) **Step I:** Face value (F) = Rs. 100, Coupon Rate = 8%,

Hence, coupon = F X Coupon Rate

= 100 X 8/100 = 8 (annual)

Step II: Market Price = 80
Step III: Current yield = Coupon / Market Price
= 8/80 = 0.1 = 10%

Hence, current yield = 10%.

(ii) **Step I**: Face value (F) = Rs. 100, Coupon Rate = 8%,

Hence, coupon = F X Coupon Rate

= 100 X 8/100 = 8 (annual)

Step II: Market Price = 80
Step III: Current yield = Coupon / Market Price
= 8/80 = 0.1 = 10%
Hence, current yield = 10%.

(iii) **Step I**: Face value (F) = Rs. 100, Coupon Rate = 8%,

Hence, coupon = F X Coupon Rate

= 100 X 8/100 = 8 (annual)

Step II: Market Price = 80

Step III: Current yield = Coupon / Market Price
= 8/80 = 0.1 = 10%
Hence, current yield = 10%.

(iv) **Step I**: Face value (F) = Rs. 100, Coupon Rate = 10%,

Hence, coupon = F X Coupon Rate

= 100 X 10/100 = 10

Step II: Market Price = 90
Step III: Current yield = Coupon / Market Price
= 10/90 = 0.111 = 11.1%

Hence, current yield = 11.1%.

(v) **Step I**: Face value (F) = Rs. 100, Coupon Rate = 10%,

Hence, coupon = F X Coupon Rate

= 100 X 10/100 = 10

Step II: Market Price = 110
Step III: Current yield = Coupon / Market Price
= 10/110 = 0.0909 = 9.09%
Hence, current yield = 9.09%.

(vi) **Step I**: Face value (F) = Rs. 1000, Coupon Rate = 8%,

Hence, coupon = F X Coupon Rate

= 1000 X 8/100 = 80

Step II: Market Price = 1100
Step III: Current yield = Coupon / Market Price
= 80/1100 = 0.0727 = 7.27%
Hence, current yield = 7.27%.

TYPE IV:
Q1. (i) **Step I**: Face value (F) = Rs. 100, Coupon Rate = 8%,

Hence, coupon = F X Coupon Rate

= 100 X 8/100 = 8 (annual)

Step II: Apply the formula:
$$90 = \frac{8}{(1+r)} + \frac{8+100}{(1+r)^2}$$
$$\Rightarrow r = 0.1383 = 13.83\%$$

Hence, YTM of bond is 13.83%.
NOTE: If Market price < Face value; YTM > Coupon rate.

(ii) **Step I**: Face value (F) = Rs. 100, Coupon Rate = 8%,

Hence, coupon = F X Coupon Rate

= 100 X 8/100 = 8 (annual)

Step II: Apply the formula:

$$100 = \frac{8 + 100}{(1 + r)}$$

⇨ 100 + 100r = 108
⇨ 100r = 8
⇨ r = 0.08 = 8%.

Hence, YTM of bond is 8%.
NOTE: If Face value = Market price; Coupon rate = YTM.

(iii) **Step I**: Face value (F) = Rs. 100, Coupon Rate = 5%,

Hence, coupon = F X Coupon Rate

= 100 X 5/100 = 5

Step II: Apply the formula:

$$100 = \frac{5 + 100}{(1 + r)}$$

⇨ 100 + 100r = 105
⇨ r = 5/100 = 0.05 = 5%.

Hence, YTM of bond is 5%.
NOTE: If Market price = Face value; Coupon rate = YTM.

(iv) **Step I**: Face value (F) = Rs. 100, Coupon Rate = 8%,

Hence, coupon = F X Coupon Rate

= 100 X 8/100 = 8 (annual)

As frequency is semi-annual, hence,

Semi-annual Coupon = C/f = 8/2 = 4.

Step II: Apply the formula:

$$80 = \frac{4}{\left(1+\frac{r}{2}\right)} + \frac{4+100}{\left(1+\frac{r}{2}\right)^2}$$

$$\Rightarrow \frac{r}{2} = 0.165$$

$$\Rightarrow r = 33\%.$$

Hence, YTM = 33%.

(v) **Step I**: Face value (F) = Rs. 100, Coupon Rate = 8%,

Hence, coupon = F X Coupon Rate

= 100 X 8/100 = 8 (annual)

Hence, quarterly coupon = 8/4 = 2.

Step II: Apply the formula:

$$95 = \frac{2}{(1+r)^{\frac{1}{4}}} + \frac{2}{(1+r)^{\frac{2}{4}}} + \frac{2}{(1+r)^{\frac{3}{4}}} + \frac{2+100}{(1+r)^{\frac{4}{4}}}$$

$$\Rightarrow r = 14\%.$$

Using short – cut method, r = 13.4%
Hence, YTM = 14%.

(vi) **Step I**: Face value (F) = Rs. 100, Coupon Rate = 10%,

Hence, coupon = F X Coupon Rate

= 100 X 10/100 = 10

Therefore, monthly coupon = C/f = 10/12.

Step II: Apply the formula:

$$90 = \frac{10/12}{(1+r)^{1/12}} + \frac{10/12}{(1+r)^{2/12}} + \ldots + \frac{10/12 + 100}{(1+r)}$$

⇨ r = 21.28% (by short-cut formula).

TYPE V:

Q1. (i) **Step I:** Face Value (F) = 100, Coupon Rate = 10%
Hence, Coupon = F x Coupon Rate = 100 x 10/100 = 10.
Step II: Market Price of bond = 90, Required Rate of Return = 8%.

Step III: $P_{calculated} = \dfrac{10}{(1+0.08)} + \dfrac{10+100}{(1+0.08)^2}$
= 103.57

Step IV: Since, $P_{calculated}$ > Market Price.
Hence, Bond is under-valued.

(ii) **Step I:** Face Value (F) = 100, Coupon Rate = 8%
Hence, Coupon = F x Coupon Rate = 100 x 8/100 = 8.
Step II: Market Price of bond = 97, Required Rate of Return = 8%.

Step III: $P_{calculated} = \dfrac{8}{(1+0.08)} + \dfrac{8+100}{(1+0.08)^2} = 100.$

Step IV: Since, $P_{calculated}$ > Market Price.
Hence, Bond is under-valued.

(iii) **Step I:** Face Value (F) = 100, Coupon Rate = 10%
Hence, Coupon = F x Coupon Rate = 100 x 10/100 = 10.
Step II: Market Price of bond = 99, Required Rate of Return = 7%.

Step III: $P_{calculated} = \dfrac{10}{(1+0.07)} + \dfrac{10}{(1+0.07)^2} + \dfrac{10+100}{(1+0.07)^3}$

= 107.87

Step IV: Since, $P_{calculated}$ > Market Price of bond.
Hence, Bond is under-valued.

(iv) **Step I:** Face Value (F) = 100, Coupon Rate = 10%
Hence, Coupon = F x Coupon Rate = 100 x 10/100 = 10.
Step II: Market Price of bond = 100, Required Rate of Return = 10%.

Step III: $P_{calculated} = \dfrac{10}{(1+0.1)} + \dfrac{10}{(1+0.1)^2} + \dfrac{10}{(1+0.1)^3} + \dfrac{10+100}{(1+0.1)^4}$

= 100.

Step IV: Since, $P_{calculated}$ = Market Price of bond.
Hence, Bond is correctly valued.

(v) **Step I:** Face Value (F) = 100, Coupon Rate = 7%
Hence, Coupon = F x Coupon Rate = 100 x 7/100 = 7.

Step II: Market Price of bond = 90, Required Rate of Return = 8%.

Step III: $P_{calculated} = \dfrac{7}{(1+0.08)} + \dfrac{7}{(1+0.08)^2} + \dfrac{7+100}{(1+0.08)^3}$

= 97.42

Step IV: Since, $P_{calculated}$ > Market Price of bond.

Hence, Bond is under – valued.

(vi) **Step I:** Face Value (F) = 100, Coupon Rate = 8%

Hence, Coupon = F x Coupon Rate = 100 x 8/100 = 8.

Step II: Market Price of bond = 110, Required Rate of Return = 12%.

Step III: $P_{calculated} = \dfrac{8}{(1+0.12)} + \dfrac{8+100}{(1+0.12)^2}$

= 93.24

Step IV: Since, $P_{calculated}$ < Market Price of bond.

Hence, Bond is over – priced.

(vii) **Step I:** Face Value (F) = 100, Coupon Rate = 10%

Hence, Coupon = F x Coupon Rate = 100 x 10/100 = 10.

Step II: Market Price of bond = 110, Required Rate of Return = 12%.

Step III: $P_{calculated} = \dfrac{10}{(1+0.12)} + \dfrac{10+100}{(1+0.12)^2}$

= 96.62

Step IV: Since, $P_{calculated}$ < Market Price of bond.

Hence, Bond is over – priced.

TYPE VI

Q1. (i) **Step I:** Face Value (F) = 100, Coupon Rate = 10%,

Coupon = Face Value x Coupon Rate = 100 x 10/100 = 10.

Step II: Conversion Ratio = 15; Price of one share on conversion = 5.

Step III: Required Rate of Return = 8%, n = 2 years.

Step IV: $P = \dfrac{10}{(1+0.08)} + \dfrac{10 + 15 \times 5}{(1+0.08)^2}$

= 82.13

Hence, correct price of convertible bond = Rs. 82.13

(ii) **Step I:** Face Value (F) = 100, Coupon Rate = 10%,

Coupon = Face Value x Coupon Rate = 100 x 10/100 = 10.

Step II: Conversion Ratio = 10; Price of one share = Rs8.

Step III: Required Rate of Return = 7%, n = 2 years.

Step IV: $P = \dfrac{10}{(1+0.07)} + \dfrac{10 + 10 \times 8}{(1+0.07)^2}$

= 87.95

Hence, correct price of one convertible bond = Rs. 87.95

(iii) **Step I:** Face Value (F) = 1000, Coupon Rate = 5%,

Coupon = Face Value x Coupon Rate = 1000 x 5/100 = 50.

Step II: Conversion Ratio = 20; Price of one share = Rs40.

Step III: Required Rate of Return = 10%, n = 3 years.

Step IV: $P = \dfrac{50}{(1+0.1)} + \dfrac{50}{(1+0.1)^2} + \dfrac{50 + 20 \times 40}{(1+0.1)^3}$

$= 725.39$

Hence, correct price of convertible bonds = Rs. 87.95

(iv) **Step I:** Face Value (F) = 1000, Coupon Rate = 15%,

Coupon = Face Value x Coupon Rate = 1000 x 15/100 = 150.

Step II: Conversion Ratio = 15; Conversion Price = Rs 50.

Step III: Required Rate of Return = 12%, n = 3 years.

Step IV: $P = \dfrac{150}{(1+0.12)} + \dfrac{150}{(1+0.12)^2} + \dfrac{150 + 15 \times 50}{(1+0.12)^3}$

$= 894.10$

Hence, correct price of convertible bond = Rs. 894.10

(v) **Step I:** Face Value (F) = 500, Coupon Rate = 10%,

Coupon = Face Value x Coupon Rate = 500 x 10/100 = 50.

Step II: Conversion Ratio = 20; Conversion Price = Rs 20.

Step III: Required Rate of Return = 8%, n = 4 years.

Step IV: $P = \dfrac{50}{(1+0.08)} + \dfrac{50}{(1+0.08)^2} + \dfrac{50}{(1+0.08)^3} + \dfrac{50 + 20 \times 20}{(1+0.08)^4}$

$= 459.62$

Hence, correct price of convertible bonds = Rs. 459.62

(vi) **Step I:** Face Value (F) = 500, Coupon Rate = 8%,

Coupon = Face Value x Coupon Rate = 500 x 8/100 = 40.

Step II: Conversion Ratio = 20; Conversion Price = Rs 22.
Step III: Required Rate of Return = 14%, n = 1 year.

Step IV: $P = \dfrac{40}{(1+0.14)} + \dfrac{20 \times 22}{(1+0.14)}$

= 421.05

Hence, correct price of convertible bonds = Rs. 421.05

(vii) **Step I:** Face Value (F) = 400, Coupon Rate = 10%,
Coupon = Face Value x Coupon Rate = 400 x 10/100 = 40.
Step II: Conversion Ratio = 20; Conversion Price = Rs 30.
Step III: Required Rate of Return = 15%, n = 2 years.

Step IV: $P = \dfrac{40}{(1+0.15)} + \dfrac{40 + 20 \times 30}{(1+0.15)^2}$

= 518.71

Hence, correct price of convertible bonds = Rs. 518.71

(viii) **Step I:** Face Value (F) = 400, Coupon Rate = 8%,
Coupon = Face Value x Coupon Rate = 400 x 8/100 = 32.
Step II: Conversion Ratio = 20; Conversion Price = Rs 10.
Step III: Required Rate of Return = 20%, n = 1 year.

Step IV: $P = \dfrac{32 + 20 \times 10}{(1.20)}$

= 193.33

Hence, price of convertible bond = Rs. 193.33

MORE PROBLEMS ON VALUATION OF BONDS

Q1. FCI Ltd. has recently issued a debenture of face value Rs. 1,000 having coupon rate of 10% p.a. payable annually. There are 3 tranches of bond:

Tranch A: Time to maturity of 10 years

Tranch B: Time to maturity of 20 years

Tranch C: Perpetual Bond

Answer the following:

a) Price of bond A, B & C. (Intrinsic value)
b) If the price (market) of Tranch A, B & C be Rs.990, Rs.1,100 and Rs. 1,000. Identify under-priced, over-priced and correctly priced Bonds.
c) Current yield of Bonds; if market prices are as given in question (b).
d) YTM (Yield to Maturity); if market prices are as given in question (b).
e) If required rate of return is 13%; should Mr. X invest in these bonds.

Required Rate of Return in all the above cases is 13%.

Q2. Write coupon flow statement of the following:

i) Face value = Rs.100, Coupon Rate = 8%, Time to Maturity = 5 years.

ii) Face value = Rs.2000, Coupon Rate = 10%, Time to Maturity = 3 years.

iii) Face value = Rs.1000, Coupon Rate = 10%, Time to Maturity = 5 years.

iv) Face value = Rs.500, Coupon Rate = 5%, Time to Maturity = 3 years.

v) Face value = Rs.1000, Coupon Rate = 15%, Time to Maturity = 5 years.

vi) Face value = Rs.700, Coupon Rate = 8%, Time to Maturity = 3 years.

Q3. Find price of bonds given in Q2; if required rate of return is 10%.

Q4. Write Cash Flow Statements in following cases:-

	FACE VALUE (Rs.)	COUPON RATE (%)	MARKET PRICE (Rs.)	Time to Maturity n (years)
(i)	1,000	8	800	2
(ii)	2,000	9	1,100	7
(iii)	500	10	100	3
(iv)	1,000	12	800	3
(v)	500	12	450	1

Q5. Find YTM (Yield to Maturity) in all given cases in Q4.

Q6. (a) Find current yield in all given cases of Q4.

(b) Identify over-valued/ under-valued / correctly priced bonds given in Q4 if required rate of return is 8%.

Q7. Find YTM of a bond having face value = Rs. 1000, coupon

rate = 10%, payable semi-annually and current market price of bond = Rs. 880, term to maturity = 3 years.

Q8. Find YTM of a bond having face value = Rs. 800, coupon rate = 8%, payable quarterly and current market price of bond = Rs. 700, term to maturity = 1 year.

Q9. Find YTM of a bond having face value = Rs. 1000, coupon rate = 10%, payable monthly and current market price of bond = Rs. 800, term to maturity = 2 years.

Q10. AA Ltd. has recently issued bonds having face value of Rs. 1000 carrying coupon rate of 8% p.a., payable annually. There are two investment options:-\

Option 1: Time to maturity of 5 years.

Option 2: Time to maturity of 1 year.

Answer the following:-

a) Intrinsic values of bonds of each option.
b) If market price of option 1 bond at the end of year 1 (after coupon payment) is Rs. 990. Verify bond is over-valued or under-valued.]
c) YTM of both bonds if market prices are Rs. 900 and Rs. 980 respectively.
d) If required rate of return of Mr. B is 12%; should he invest in option 1 bond?
e) Current yield of bonds of market price are as given in (c).

Required rate of return in all above cases is 12%.

Q11. A convertible bond having face value of Rs.1000 carrying 10% coupon rate is trading at Rs.900. Term to maturity is 3 years. The conversion ratio is 1:20 i.e. for 1 bond 20 equities. Expected price of equity on the day of conversion is Rs.25. Find YTM of the bond.

Q12. A convertible bond having face value of Rs.1000 carrying 15% coupon rate payable semi-annually is trading at Rs.900. Term to maturity is 2 years. The conversion ratio is 1:15 i.e. for 1 bond 15 equities. Expected price of equity on the day of conversion is Rs.60. Find YTM of the bond.

Q13. Find YTM of following convertible bonds:

Face value of each bond = Rs.800

i. Coupon rate = 10%; Term to maturity = 2 years; Conversion Ratio = 1:20; Conversion price = Rs. 40; Current market price of bond = Rs.850.
ii. Coupon rate = 5%; Term to maturity = 3 years; Conversion Ratio = 1:30; Conversion price = Rs. 30; Current market price of bond = Rs.780.
iii. Coupon rate = 10%; Term to maturity = 2 years; Conversion Ratio = 1:20; Conversion price = Rs. 40; Current market price of bond = Rs.700.

iv. Coupon rate = 8%; Term to maturity = 2 years; Conversion Ratio = 1:30; Conversion price = Rs. 20; Current market price of bond = Rs.560.

v. Coupon rate = 15%; Term to maturity = 7 years; Conversion Ratio = 1:40; Conversion price = Rs. 20; Current market price of bond = Rs.700.

Q14. Calculate Intrinsic Value (price) of following bonds:

i. Face value = Rs.1000; Coupon Rate = 10%; Term to maturity = 2 years; Required Rate of Return = 10%.

ii. Face value = Rs.1000; Coupon Rate = 10%; Term to maturity = 3 years; Required Rate of Return = 8%.

iii. Face value = Rs.700; Coupon Rate = 9%, Payable semi-annually; Term to maturity = 2 years; Required Rate of Return = 9%.

5 COST OF CAPITAL

Objective : To enable readers to understand the calculation of cost of different sources of capitals and then overall cost of capital.

Cost of capital : Companies use different sources of finance to meet its investment need. The proportion of capital may be different for different sources. Hence, we will have to use weighted average to calculate the overall cost of capital.

Hence, cost of capital is the minimum rate of return that a company must earn from its investment to meet the obligations of providers of different sources of funds (investors /creditors).

Sources of Long- term finance : Different sources of long term finances are : Term-loan, debentures, equity and preferential-shares.

Cost of Term-loan : If I is the rate of interest paid on term loan, then I(1-T) will be the effective cost of term loan; because interest paid on term loan is a tax deductible item.

Hence, Cost of term loan = I(1-T). (also known as effective cost of Term loan)

Here, T = Tax rate.

Cost of Debentures : As interest paid on debenture is also a tax deductible item and hence, effective cost of debenture can be given as :

$$\text{Price}(P) = \frac{C(1-T)}{(1+K_d)} + \frac{C(1-T)}{(1+K_d)^2} + \ldots + \frac{C(1-T)+F}{(1+K_d)^n}$$

C = coupon, K_d = cost of debt

Using approximation formula explained in chapter 5, we have,

$$K_d = \frac{C(1-T) + (F-P)/n}{(0.4 \times F + 0.6 \times P)}$$

Cost of Equity : Cost of equity is identified using dividend discount model:

$$P = \frac{D_1}{(1+K_e)} + \frac{D_2}{(1+K_e)^2} + \ldots + \frac{D_n}{(1+K_e)^n}$$

If dividend paid is different in different years.

Or

By using constant growth model; if the growth rate is constant :

$$P = \frac{D_1}{(K_e - g)}$$

Or

By using CAPM model :

$R = R_f + \beta [R_m - R_f]$

Cost of Preferential Shares :

In Preferential shares cash inflows are dividends and principal amount and hence, cost of preferential share can be given as :

$$P = \frac{D}{(1+K_p)} + \frac{D}{(1+K_p)^2} + \ldots + \frac{D+F}{(1+K_p)^n}$$

Above equation is similar to bond valuation equation and hence its approximate value can also be given as :

$$K = \frac{D + (F-P)/n}{(0.4 \times F + 0.6 \times P)}$$

Cost of Retained Earnings : Since retained earnings is viewed as an additional capital supplied by common share holders and hence cost of equity should be equal to cost of retained earnings.

$K_e = K_r$

But cost of retained earnings should ideally be less than cost of new issued equity capital because of saving of floatation cost in case of retained earnings. Hence,

$$K_{ex} = \frac{Ke}{(1-f)}$$

f = floatation cost as a % of current market price.

where K_{ex} = cost of external equity.

Weighted Average Cost of Capital (WACC) : In any project, different sources of finance is used and hence, we must calculate the weighted average cost of capital (WACC).

$$WACC = We*Ke + W_d*K_d + W_p*K_p + Wr*Kr.$$

Where We = weight of equity

Wd = weight of debt

W_f = weight of preferential share

Wr = weight of retained earnings.

Type I – Problems based on cost of Term Loan :-

Step I : Identify the rate of interest being charged on term loan (I).

Step II : Identify the corporate Tax rate (T).

Step III : Apply the formula :

    Effective cost of Term loan = I(1-T).

Ex 1: Find the effective cost of term loan of company XYZ Ltd. if it raises term loan at an interest rate of 15% per annum and the corporate tax rate is 30%.

Sol : Step I : Given rate of interest of term loan (I) = 15%.

Step II : Corporate Tax rate (T) = 30%

Step III : Effective cost of Term loan

$$= I(1-T)$$
$$= 15(1 - 0.3) = 10.5\%.$$

Hence, effective cost of term loan = 10.5%.

Practice Problems

Q1. Company ABC Ltd. has raised a term loan of Rs.1 crore at a rate of 20% per annum. The corporate tax is 30%. Find the effective cost of term loan.

Q2. A company has raised a term loan at a rate of 10% per annum. The corporate tax rate is 35%. Find the effective cost of term loan.

Q3. If the effective cost of term loan of a company is 12% and corporate tax rate is 30%. Find the cost of term loan at which it was raised.

Q4. Identify the better option of financing from the given two :

(a) A term loan at the rate of 8% per annum compounded half-yearly.
(b) A term loan at the rate of 6% per annum compounded quarterly.

Assume a corporate tax rate of 30%.

Type II : Problems based on cost of Debentures.

Step I : Identify/Calculate coupon, market price of bond, corporate tax rate.

Step II : Identify face value of bond and term to maturity of the bond.

Step III : Apply the formula :

$$P = \frac{C(1-T)}{(1+K_d)} + \frac{C(1-T)}{(1+K_d)^2} + \ldots + \frac{C(1-T)+F}{(1+K_d)^n}$$

Calculate K_d which is cost of debenture.

By applying following formula, an approx. value of K_d can be calculated :

$$K_d = \frac{D + (F-P)/n}{(0.4 \times F + 0.6 \times P)}$$

Ex1 : A bond of face value of Rs.1000 having a coupon of 10% per annum was issued on 4 March 2012. The term to maturity of the bond is 5 years. The market price of bond is Rs.900 and corporate tax is 30%. Find the cost of debenture.

Sol : Step I : Coupon = 1000*10/100 = 100

Market Price (P) = 900

Tax rate = 30%

Step II : Face value (F) = 1000

Term to maturity (n) = 5

Step III : Apply the formula :

$$900 = \frac{100(1-0.3)}{(1+K_d)} + \frac{100(1-0.3)}{(1+K_d)^2} + \ldots + \frac{100(1-0.3)+1000}{(1+K_d)^5}$$

Hence, K_d = 9.57%. (Using approximate formula)

Practice Problems

Q1. Find the cost of debenture in the following case :

S.No.	Face Value($)	Coupon Rate	Market Price ($)	Time to Maturity (Years)	Tax Rate
I	1000	15%	800	5	30%
Ii	100	10%	90	10	35%
Iii	100	8%	90	5	30%
Iv	1000	12%	900	15	30%
V	100	8%	70	10	30%

Type III : Problems based on cost of Preferential Shares :

Step I : Identify the value of dividend, face value and market price of preferential shares.

Step II : Identify the period before redemption (n).

Step III : Apply the formula :

$$K_p = \frac{D + (F-P)/n}{(0.4 \times F + 0.6 \times P)}$$

K_p is cost of preferential share.

Ex1 : Company XYZ Ltd. has issued a preferential share of face value of Rs.1000, carrying a dividend of Rs.80 per year. It will be redeemable after 5 years at par. The market price of preferential share is (i.e. value realized) Rs.1100. Find the cost of preferential share.

Sol: Step I : Dividend (D) = Rs.80

Face value (F) = Rs.1000

Market price (P) = Rs.1100

Step II : n = 5 years

Step III : Apply formula :

$$Kp = \frac{D + (F-P)/n}{(0.4 \times F + 0.6 \times P)} = \frac{80 + (1000-1100)/5}{(0.4 \times 1000 + 0.6 \times 1100)}$$

Kp = 5.66%

Hence, cost of preferential share = 5.66%.

Practice Problems

Q1. Find the cost of preferential share in the following cases, face value of share is Rs.100 in each case :

Dividend(Rs.) payable annually	Market price (Rs.)	Redeemable after(years)
(i) 10	90	10
(ii) 20	110	10

(iii) 50   80   5

(iv)   5   90   20

Q2. A company has issued preferential share of face value Rs.1000, having dividend 12% per annum is redeemable at a premium of Rs.20 after 10 years. Find cost of preferential share if the market value of share is Rs.900.

Type IV : Problems based on cost of retained earnings and External equity.

Step I : Identify/Calculate cost of Equity.

Step II : Identify floatation cost.

Step III : Apply following formula :

$$Kr = Ke \; ; \quad Kr = \text{cost of retained earning}$$

& $Kex = Ke/1 - f$; Kex = cost of external equity.

Ex1 : A company has current cost of equity as 15%. The cost of issuing external equity is 8.1%. Find cost of retained earning and cost of external equity.

Sol : Step I : Cost of Equity (Ke) = 15%

Step II : Floatation cost = 8%

Step III : Cost of retained earning Kr = Ke = 15%

Cost of external equity = Ke/1- f = 15%/1 − 0.08

= 16.3%.

As cost of retained earning is lower than cost of external equity. Hence, a company should use retained earning as source of finance.

Practice Problems

Q1. Find cost of retained earning and external equity in the following cases. Also, interpret the result:

	Cost of Equity	Floatation Cost (as a % of current market price)
(i)	10%	12%
(ii)	10%	30%
(iii)	10%	90%
(iv)	20%	20%

Type V : Problems based on WACC.

Step I : Identify/Calculate the costs of all sources of finance independently.

Step II : Identify/Calculate weightage of each source of finance (capital).

Step III : Apply the formula:

$$WACC = We*Ke + Wd*Kd + Wr*Kr + Wp*Kp.$$

Ex1 : A company has the following sources of finance :

Source	Weightage	Cost
Equity	50%	10%

Debenture	30%	8% after tax
Retained earning	10%	10%
Preferential share	5%	12%
Term loan	5%	6% after tax

Step I : Sources of finance & costs are already indicated.

Step II : Weights are given.

Step III : Apply the formula :

$$WACC = 0.5*10\% + 0.3*8\% + 0.1*10\% + 0.05*12\% + 0.05*6\%.$$

$$WACC = 9.3\%.$$

Note : K_d, K_l must be after tax. If given values are before tax, adjust if for tax as,

$K'_d = K_d * (1- T)$

$K'_l = K_l * (1- T)$

Here, T = tax rate

K'_d, K'_l = before tax

Ex : Before tax, cost of debt is 10%; tax rate is 40%. Find post – tax cost of debt.

$K'_d = K_d * (1- T) = 10\% (1- 0.4) = 6\%.$

Therefore, Post – tax cost of debt is 6%.

Practice Problems

Q1. Company XYZ Ltd. uses following capital structure. Find weighted average cost of capital.

Source	Weight	Cost
Equity	40%	20%
Term loan	60%	10% (after tax)

[Hint : As only two sources; hence, Wp, W_l & Wr = 0]

Q2. Find WACC in the following case, if tax rate is 30%,

Source	Weight	Cost
Debenture	50%	20% post - tax

Q3. Find WACC in the following cases; if tax rate is 30%;

	Source	Weight	Cost
CASE 1:	Equity	70%	10%
	Retained earning	20%	10%
	Pref. share	10%	12%
CASE 2:	Equity	50%	15%
	Debenture	30%	10% post-tax
	Term Loan	20%	20% pre-tax
CASE 3:	Equity	40%	20%
	Retained earnings	30%	20%
	Pref. share	10%	15%

	Debenture	10%	10% post-tax
	Term Loan	10%	12% pre-tax
CASE 4:	Equity	40%	20%
	Term Loan	30%	30% pre-tax
	Debenture	30%	10% post-tax
CASE 5:	Debenture	40%	20% pre-tax
	Term Loan	30%	15% pre-tax
	Pref. share	10%	10%
	Equity	20%	15%

Also, select the best capital structure on the basis of WACC.

6 CAPITAL BUDGETING

- **Capital Budgeting:** Capital budgeting is the process of allocating funds for long-term investments. Hence, capital budgeting deals with long-term investments only.
- **Net Present Value (NPV) Method:** NPV of a project is the net sum of all the present values of all cash flows.
- **NPV= Present Value of cash inflows – Present value of cash outflows**

$$NPV = \sum_{t=1}^{n} \frac{C_t}{(1+r)^t} - initial\,investment$$

C_t is cash inflows at the end of the tth year.

r = discount rate

n = life of the project.

- **IRR (Internal Rate of Return):** IRR is the rate of return that a project earns on its entire life. It is also explained as the rate at which NPV of a project is zero.

$$NPV = \sum_{t=1}^{n} \frac{C_t}{(1+r)^t} - initial\,investment$$

$$0 = \sum_{t=1}^{n} \frac{C_t}{(1+r)^t} - initial\,investment$$

⇨ Initial Investment = $\sum_{t=1}^{n} \frac{C_t}{(1+r)^t}$

⇨ Here **r** is the internal rate of return.

- **Modified IRR:** A project may have cash outflows at different point in time and hence, giving more than one value of IRR. This makes managers confused while taking decisions about the correct value of IRR.

  Modified IRR overcomes with this problem. Since, the problem with IRR was cash outflows at more than one time period. So, if we can bring all cash flows (outflows and inflows) at one time period then the problem of IRR can be removed. So, procedure will be:

(i) Find present value of all cash outflows:

$$\text{Present Value} = \sum_{t=0}^{n} \frac{C_t}{(1+r)^t}$$

(ii) Find terminal value of all cash inflows

$$\text{Terminal Value (TV)} = \sum_{t=0}^{n} CashInflows \times (1+r)^{n-t}$$

(iii) Now discount TV to bring it at present.

$$\text{Present Value of TV} = \frac{TV}{(1+MIRR)^n}$$

Since, at IRR, PV of cash inflows = PV of cash outflows

Hence, $PV = PV$ of $TV = \dfrac{TV}{(1+MIRR)^n}$

Here, MIRR is the modified rate of return.

- **Accounting Rate of Return:** Accounting rate of return is also known as average rate of return. It is expressed as:

$$\frac{Profit After Tax (PAT)}{Book Value of Investment}$$

- **Payback Period:** As the name suggests; it is the time period required to re-cover the investment made. Hence, shorter the payback time period, better the project.

- **Discounted Payback Period:** The major drawback of back period is that it doesn't take time value of money into consideration. Discounted payback period is the time period required to recover the investment made taking time value of money into consideration.

- Criteria to select a project:

  a). **NPV Method:-**

  (i) If NPV > 0 ; Accept the project
  (ii) If NPV < 0 ; Reject the project
  (iii) If NPV = 0; Indifferent

  b). **IRR Method:-**

  (i) If IRR > Cost of Capital;   Accept the project

  (ii) If IRR < Cost of Capital;   Reject the project

  (iii) If IRR = Cost of Capital;   Indifferent

Type I: Problems Based on NPV

Step I: Arrange given cash flows as given:

Time	0	1	2	3	-----
Cash flows	-100	200	200	200	------

Step 2: Identify discount rate and find NPV as:

NPV = Cash outflows + PV of cash inflows

$$NPV = -100 + \frac{200}{(1+r)} + \frac{200}{(1+r)^2} + ----- \quad \text{[for all given cash flows]}$$

Step 3: If NPV >0 ; Accept the project

If NPV <0 ; Reject the project

If NPV = 0; Indifferent

Example 1: Find NPV of the project having given below cash flows:

Time	0	1	2	3	4
Cash flows	-10000	2000	2000	8000	8000

The expected rate of return is 10% per annum.

Step 1: Arrange all cash flows:

time	0	1	2	3	4
Cash flows	-10000	2000	2000	8000	8000

Step 2: Discount rate =10%. Hence,

NPV= =

$$-10000 + \frac{2000}{(1+0.1)} + \frac{2000}{(1+0.1)^2} + \frac{8000}{(1+0.1)^3} + \frac{8000}{(1+0.1)^4}$$

NPV = -10000 + 1818.18 + 1652.89 + 6010.52 + 5464.11

⇨ NPV = 4945.4

Step 3: As NPV > 0 hence, accept the project.

Practice Problems

Q1. Find NPV in the following cases if required rate of return is 15% per annum.

Case I:

time	0	1	2	3	4
Cash flows	-2000	4000	3000	2000	800

Case II:

time	0	1	2	3
Cash flows	-10000	2000	7000	800

Case III:

time	0	1	2	3	4	5
Cash flows	-20000	-4000	6000	6000	6000	6000

Case IV:

time	0	1	2	3	4	5
Cash flows	-10000	300	200	8000	12000	400

Q2. Find NPV of a project having following cash flows:

time	0	1	2	3
Cash flows	-10000	200	400	40000

The required rate of return is 2% per month.

Q3. An automatic shoe polish machine costs Rs.1,00,000. What should be the minimum annual cash inflows to make purchase of machine worthwhile? The cost of capital is 8% per annum and the life of machine is 10 years.

Q4. An automatic dry cleaner cost Rs. 10,000 and the annual cash flows is Rs. 1000 for 20 years. What is the cost of capital if you are indifferent of making investment decision?

Type II : Problems based on IRR

Step 1: Arrange cash flows as below:

time	0	1	2	3
Cash flows	-10000	200	400	40000

Step 2: Calculate NPV as

NPV = PV of cash inflows – PV of cash outflows

$$NPV = \frac{200}{(1+r)^1} + \frac{400}{(1+r)^2} + \frac{40000}{(1+r)^3} - 10000$$

Step 3: Make NPV = 0 [Since at IRR, NPV =0]

$$0= \frac{200}{(1+r)^1} + \frac{400}{(1+r)^2} + \frac{40000}{(1+r)^3} - 10000$$

Calculate **r** by trial and error method. This **r** is the internal rate of return

Example 1: A project needs Rs. 1,000 as cash outflow at the beginning of the period and it is estimated that it will provide Rs. 2,000 cash inflow for 2 years.

(a) Find IRR of the project
(b) If cost of capital of the project is 10%; what will be your decision regarding investment in this project?

Solution:

Step 1: Cash flow can be given as:

Time	0	1	2
Cash Flow	-1000	2000	2000

Step 2: NPV = PV of cash inflows – PV of cash outflows

$$\text{NPV} = \frac{2000}{(1+r)^1} + \frac{2000}{(1+r)^2} - 10000$$

Step 3: at IRR, NPV = 0

$$0 = \frac{2000}{(1+r)^1} + \frac{2000}{(1+r)^2} - 10000$$

⇨ $r = 1.732$
⇨ **Therefore, IRR = 173.20%**

(a) IRR of the project = 173.20 %

(b) Since, criteria for project selection is
If IRR > Cost of capital; Accept the project
Since, IRR = 173.20 % while cost of capital is 10%. Hence, we should accept the project.

Practice Problems

Q1. Find IRR in following cases:

Case 1:

Time	0	1	2	3
Cash Flow	-10000	3000	4000	10000

Case 2:

Time	0	1	2	3
Cash Flow	-5000	3000	3000	3000

Case 3:

Time	0	1	2
Cash Flow	-4000	2000	6000

Case 4:

Time	0	1	2	3	4
Cash Flow	-50000	2000	10000	20000	70000

Q2. A project needs Rs. 5,000 as initial investment and cash inflows are Rs. 1,000, Rs. 2,000 and Rs. 10,000 respectively in year 1, 2 and 3. Find:

(a) IRR of the project.

(b) If cost of capital of project is 80%, will you invest in this project?

Q3. Cash flows for a project is given below:

Time	0	1	2
Cash Flow	-10000	8000	4000

Find IRR of the project. Interpret the result.

Q4. Cash flows of a project is as below:

Time	0	1	2
Cash Flow	-10000	4000	8000

(a) Find IRR of the project.

(b) Compare the answer with Q3. What is your interpretation?

Q5. Cash flows for a project is as below:

Time	0	1	2	3	4
Cash Flow	-10000	2000	-2000	15000	40000

Find IRR of the project. Comment on the answer.

Type III: Problems based on Modified IRR

Step 1: Find present value of all cash outflows as

$$\text{Present Value} = \sum_{t=0}^{n} \frac{C_t}{(1+r)^t} \quad \text{------(i)}$$

Where, C_t is cash outflows.

Step 2: Find terminal value of all cash inflows:

$$\text{Terminal Value (TV)} = \sum_{t=0}^{n} CashInflows \times (1+r)^{n-t} \quad \text{--------(ii)}$$

Step 3: Now discount TV to bring it at present as:

$$\text{Present Value of TV} = \frac{TV}{(1+MIRR)^n} \quad \text{--------(iii)}$$

Step 4: Now equate equation (i) and (iii) i.e.

$$PV = \frac{TV}{(1+MIRR)^n}$$

Step 5: Calculate MIRR from above equation.

Practice Problems

Q1. Find MIRR in the following cases, if cost of capital is 10% in all cases.

(a)

Time (Years)	0	1	2	3	4
Cash Flows ($)	-10,000	-2,000	10,000	20,000	40,000

(b)

Time (Years)	0	1	2	3	4
Cash Flows ($)	-2,000	4,000	-2,000	6,000	10,000

(C)

Time (Years)	0	1	2	3	4
Cash Flows($)	-3,000	10,000	10,000	-2,000	70,000

(d)

Time (Years)	0	1	2	3	4
Cash Flows($)	-10,000	-2,000	70,000	60,000	3,000

Q2. An insurance company has launched two new policies. Evaluate the better option using MIRR concept.

Option 1: Pay premium of $ 2,000 and $7,000 in year 0 and year 2 respectively an get annual income of $ 10,000 for next 5 years after year 2.

Option 2: Pay premium of $ 7,000 and $ 2,0000 in year 0 and year 2 respectively and get annual income of $ 5,000 for next 7 years after year 2.

All other conditions remain same fir both the policies. The cost of capital is 15%.

Q3. The annual income scheme of a mutual fund is as below:
Pay annually $ 10,000 for 2 years and get annual income of $3,000 for next 7 years, irrespective of market conditions.
The cost of capital is 20%. Find MIRR of the scheme. What will be your decision as an investor?

Type IV: Problems based on payback period.

Step 1: Identify the cash outflows and inflows.

Step 2: Take summation of cash inflows till the moment (years) cash outflows= cash inflows.

Step 3: The year when cash outflows = cash inflows, is the

payback period.

Special Case: When (Cash Inflows)$_{(t-1)}$ < Cash Outflows but
(Cash Inflows)$_{(t)}$ > Cash Outflows

Calculate monthly cash inflows by dividing the given annual cash flows of year t by 12 and then find the month when cash inflows = cash outflows.

Ex1. Find payback period of the project having cash flows as below:

Time (Years)	0	1	2	3	4	5
Cash Flows ($)	-20,000	2,000	8,000	10,000	3,000	2,000

Sol:

Step 1: Cash Outflows = $ 20,000

Step 2: Summation of cash inflows of year 1,2 and 3 = $ 20,000

Step 3: At year 3 , cash outflows = cash inflows

Hence, 3 years is the payback period of this project.

Ex 2. Find payback period of the project having cash flows as below:

Time (Years)	0	1	2	3	4	5
Cash Flows($)	-20,000	2,000	8,000	24,000	3,000	2,000

Sol:

Step 1: Cash Outflows = $ 20,000

Step 2: Summation of cash inflows of year 1 and 2 = $ 10,000

Summation of cash inflows of year 1,2 and 3 = $ 34,000

Step 3: Monthly cash inflow in year 3 = 24,000/12 = $ 2,000

Step 4: Summation of cash inflows of year 1 and 2 = $ 10,000

Hence, remaining cash inflows required to make it equal to cash outflows = $ 20,000- $10,000 = $ 10,000

Since, monthly cash inflows during year 3 is $2,000 and hence, to recover $10,000, it will take 5 months more.

Hence, payback period = 2 years and 5 Months.

Ex 3. Find payback period of the project having cash flows as below:

Time (Years)	0	1	2	3	4	5
Cash Flows($)	-20,000	3,000	8,000	2,000	20,000	2,000

Sol:

Step 1: : Cash Outflows = $ 20,000

Step 2: Summation of cash inflows of year 1,2 and 3 = $ 13,000

Summation of cash inflows of year 1,2,3 and 4 = $ 33,000

Step 3: Monthly cash inflow in year 4 = 20,000/12 = $ 1,666.67

Step 4: Summation of cash inflows of year 1 and 2 = $ 10,000

Hence, remaining cash inflows required to make it equal to cash outflows = $ 20,000- $13,000 = $ 7,000

Since, monthly cash inflows during year 4 is $1,666.67 and hence, to recover $7,000, it will take 7,000/1,666.67 = 4.2 months more.

4.2 Months = 4 Months + 0.2 Months = 4Months + 0.2×30 days =

4 Months and 6 Days.

Hence, payback period = 3 years 4 Months and 6 Days.

Practice Problems

Q1. Find payback period of the project having cash flows as below:

(a)

Time (Years)	0	1	2	3	4	5	6
Cash Flows($)	-70,000	10,000	20,000	20,000	20,000	2,000	2,000

(b)

Time (Years)	0	1	2	3	4	5	6
Cash Flows($)	-20,000	8,000	8,000	8,000	8,000	8,000	8,000

(c)

Time (Years)	0	1	2	3	4	5	6
Cash Flows($)	-80,000	20,000	20,000	30,000	30,000	2,000	2,000

Q2. Find the best project based on payback period concept:

Project A:

Time (Years)	0	1	2	3	4	5
Cash Flows($)	-20,000	2,000	9,000	7,000	7,000	7,000

Project B:

Time (Years)	0	1	2	3	4	5
Cash Flows($)	-20,000	9,000	7,000	7,000	2,000	2,000

Project C:

Time (Years)	0	1	2	3	4	5
Cash Flows($)	-20,000	8,000	8,000	8,000	4,000	4,000

Q3. Based on the concept of payback period, evaluate following projects:

	Cash Flows	
Time (Years)	Project A	Project B
0	-70,000	-70,000
1	7,000	10,000
2	10,000	20,000
3	20,000	80,000
4	80,000	90,000
5	2,000	20,000
6	6,000	20,000
7	3,000	20,000
8	1,000	20,000
9	9,000	20,000
10	1,000	20,000

Also, identify the problems with payback period approach supporting your points on the basis of given data.

Q4. Based on the concept of payback period, evaluate following projects:

	Cash Flows	
Time (Years)	Project A	Project B
0	-70,000	-1,00,000

1	7,000	30,000
2	3,000	10,400
3	70,000	59,600
4	1,000	20,000
5	2,000	10,000
6	8,000	20,000
7	2,000	20,000

Also, identify the problems with payback period approach supporting your points on the basis of given data.

Type V: Problems based on "Discounted Payback Period"

Step 1: Identify cash outflows and inflows.

Step 2: Find present value of cash inflows

Step 3: Take summation of present values of cash inflows till the moment (years) cash outflow = cash inflow

Step 4: The year when cash outflow = cash inflow, is the discounted payback period.

Ex1. Find discounted payback period of the project having cash flows as below:

Time (Years)	0	1	2	3	4	5	6
Cash Flows($)	-20,000	2,000	8,000	10,000	3,000	2,000	2,000

The required rate of return is 10%

Sol:

Step 1: Cash Outflow = $20,000

Step 2: Present Value of cash inflows

Time (Years)	0	1	2	3	4	5	6
Cash Flows($)	20,000	2,000	8,000	10,000	3,000	2,000	2,000
PV of Cash Inflows		1818.18	6611.57	7513.15	2049.04	1241.84	1128.95

Present Value (PV) can be calculated as $\dfrac{CashInflow}{(1+0.10)^{time}}$

Step 3: Summation of Cash Inflows:

Cash Inflows till year 5 = 19,233.78 < 20,000

Cash Inflows till year 6 = 20,362.73 > 20,000

Hence, we will have to follow condition of "Special Case" i.e. by dividing cash inflows of year 6 by 12.

Hence, monthly cash flow in year 6 = 1,128.95/12 = 98.08

The balance amount (inflows) required in 6th year to make cash outflow = cash inflows is

20,000-19,233.78 = $ 766.22

Hence, months required to recover this amount = 766.22/98.08 = 7.8 Months

Hence, discounted payback period is 5 years and 7.8 Months i.e. 5 Years 7 Months and 24 Days.

Practice Problems

Q1. Find discounted payback period in following cases:

Case 1:

Time (Years)	0	1	2	3	4	5
Cash Flows($)	-10,000	1,000	7,000	20,000	3,000	7,000

Case 2:

Time (Years)	0	1	2	3	4	5
Cash Flows($)	-20,000	20,000	7,000	2,000	3,000	7,000

Case 3:

Time (Years)	0	1	2	3	4	5
Cash Flows($)	-5,000	2,000	3,000	7,000	8,000	7,000

Q2. Find the best project based on discounted payback period concept.

Time (Years)	Cash Flows of Project			
	A	B	C	D
0	-70,000	-70,000	-70,000	-70,000
1	70,000	2,000	10,000	2,000
2	2,000	70,000	2,000	10,000
3	10,000	10,000	70,000	70,000
4	10,000	10,000	10,000	10,000
5	10,000	10,000	10,000	10,000
6	10,000	10,000	10,000	10,000

Also comment on the results.

Q3. Find the best project based on discounted payback period concept.

	Cash Flows of Project	
Time	A	B

(Years)		
0	-20,000	-20,000
1	2,000	8,000
2	8,000	12,000
3	12,000	2,000
4	15,000	15,000
5	20,000	20,000
6	20,000	20,000

Also comment on the results.

ABOUT THE AUTHOR

Rajni Kant Rajhans is currently working as Assistant Professor-Finance with Amity University. He is also, faculty co-coordinator of "Centre for Financial Analytics" at Amity Business School, AUH. His research area includes financial economics including financial markets integration, risk premium identification etc. He has presented papers in various national as well as international conferences. There are seven research papers published to his credit in various refereed journal of repute. He is also associated with many national and international journals as a reviewer. He can be contacted at **rajnikantrajhans@gmail.com**.

www.ingramcontent.com/pod-product-compliance
Lightning Source LLC
Chambersburg PA
CBHW071013200526
45171CB00007B/119